W9-BRV-305

The Dividend Rich
Investor

About the Authors

Joseph Tigue is Managing Editor of Standard & Poor's investment advisory newsletter, *The Outlook*, as well as Editor of S&P's *Directory of Dividend Reinvestment Plans*. Mr. Tigue's frequent appearances in the business media include NBC, CNBC, CNN, PBS, the BBC, and various radio shows. He lives in Westbury, New York.

Joseph Lisanti is Senior Editor of Standard & Poor's *The Outlook*. Prior to joining S&P in 1989, Mr. Lisanti was Senior Editor of *Physicians Financial News* and Managing Editor of *Fact: The Money Management Magazine*. He lives in New York City and Great Barrington, Massachusetts.

The Dividend Rich Investor

Building Wealth with High-Quality, Dividend-Paying Stocks

Revised and Updated

Joseph Tigue
Joseph Lisanti

McGraw-Hill

New York   San Francisco   Washington, D.C.   Auckland   Bogotá
Caracas   Lisbon   London   Madrid   Mexico City   Milan
Montreal   New Delhi   San Juan   Singapore
Sydney   Tokyo   Toronto

McGraw-Hill

A Division of The **McGraw·Hill** Companies

1 2 3 4 5 6 7 8 9 0 DOC/DOC 9 0 3 2 1 0 9 8

ISBN 0-07-064753-4

The editors for this book were Susan Barry and Griffin Hansbury, the editing supervisor was Fred Dahl, and the production supervisor was Sherri Souffrance. It was set in Caslon 540 by Inkwell Publishing Services.

Printed and bound by R. R. Donnelley & Sons Company.

McGraw-Hill books are available at special quantity discounts to use as premiums and sales promotions, or for use in corporate training programs. For more information, please write to the Director of Special Sales, McGraw-Hill, 11 West 19th Street, New York, NY 10011. Or contact your local bookstore.

Contents

Foreword

Investors these days like having things done for them. The mutual fund manager selects the stocks and times the purchases after the 401(k) plan automatically deducts the money from the investors' paychecks.

Now, if you do buy stocks directly, the companies in which you have an ownership interest are telling you that they know better what to do with the fruits of your investment than you do. The latest trend among U.S. corporations is to pay out as little as possible to you in dividends and instead use the cash as *they* see fit. The payout ratio—dividends as a percentage of earnings—has fallen to one of the lowest levels in history. And that's not because the economy is on the brink of disaster, so that companies have to hoard cash. Profits are running at record levels.

If you've wondered why stock yields are so meager, a good part of the reason is low payout ratios. The other part, of course, is high stock prices. As of July 1998, the yield of the S&P 500 index was less than one-third the average of 4.4% in the 72 years from 1926 to 1997. It had been under 2% since January 1997 and under 3% since October 1992, or for nearly six years. Before that, the yield had never gotten below 2.64% (August 1987 and January 1973), while the longest continuous period of sub-3% yields was January 1972 through May 1973, or one and a third years.

To be fair, by retaining a huge part of its earnings, the corporation you invest in often does have your best interests in mind. It's trying to enhance the value of your shares through what it regards as an attractive opportunity to invest in the company itself or in the company's stock in the open market (share buybacks).

A low payout policy is also good for corporate managers. They benefit, as you would, if the shares rise in price, thanks to options and executive compensation tied to stock performance. They also love the flexibility of being able to deploy corporate earnings when and how they choose—buying in shares, paying down debt, building plants, making acquisitions, and the like.

To a large degree, however, what the company is offering you, the shareholder, is a promise. It is saying it will invest profitably for you money that would otherwise go straight into your pocket. That's worked well as the stock market has soared. As you've watched the prices of your shares climb, you've been able to tell yourself that the dividends you've lost out on haven't been missed and that, at the same time, you've been tax-wise. (Dividends are taxed as ordinary income in the year received. Appreciation is taxed at a usually lower capital gains rate—and then only when you sell the shares.)

But don't forget the "a bird in the hand" adage. If stock prices level off or decline for a time, the dividend will prove to be your friend. Maybe you want to use dividends to pay monthly bills. Or perhaps you prefer to be the one to decide when and by how much to increase your investment in a particular company, if at all—and not leave that choice to the company. If you do want to increase your investment, generally it's as simple as enrolling in the company's dividend reinvestment plan. If you don't, you should be entitled to a reasonable and growing dividend.

The coauthors of this book, Joseph Tigue and Joseph Lisanti, have seen the investment winds shift more than a few times. They know the difference between fads and time-tested investment concepts. They are especially aware of how some big, big nest eggs have developed from years of expanding dividend income. Joe and Joe bring to this work a combined total of more than forty years of experience, much of it in researching, writing, and editing feature articles for one of the oldest and most successful investment advisory publications, Standard & Poor's *The Outlook*. They'll give you some excellent advice on how to make dividends work for you.

ARNOLD M. KAUFMAN
Editor, *The Outlook*

Acknowledgments

Although writing a book has often been described as a lonely pursuit, we have been fortunate to have a group of knowledgeable people always available to discuss various ideas and concepts that ultimately found their way into this work. We thank them for their efforts, without which this book would be poorer.

Many of our colleagues at Standard & Poor's have been generous in offering a helping hand at numerous points along the creative path: Jim Dunn and Arnold Kaufman read over the manuscript and offered helpful suggestions on how to make it better and clearer. Chris Peng worked hard, as she always does, to create the charts that grace these pages. Howard Silverblatt tweaked the vast S&P databases to provide us with numerous tables of interesting stocks. David Braverman did the pioneering work on electric utilities stocks that we built upon in Chapter 8. Carol Fitzgerald, Rick Perdew, and Richard ZainEldeen located the sometimes obscure materials that we needed to complete our research.

We would also like to thank Bruce Agostino of the New York Stock Exchange, Katrina Clay of the American Stock Exchange, Robert Cohen of First Call, Ed Keon of I/B/E/S, and Bill Wink of Nasdaq for providing information on the services available from their organizations.

Thanks to Fred Dahl for his extraordinary attention to detail in turning our manuscript into a book. Our patient editors at McGraw-Hill, David Conti and Allyson Arias, never once laughed at our outrageous predictions of how little time it would take to write this book. They have our thanks for that. A special thanks to Susan Barry and Griffin Hansbury at McGraw-Hill for making this softcover edition a reality.

We would also like to thank our wives, Barbara Tigue and Judith Cooperstein Lisanti, whose understanding and support made this book possible.

J.T. & J.L.
New York

The Dividend Rich Investor

Introduction

Most people have financial goals in life. Since you are reading this book, we assume you do, too. Maybe you want to set aside enough money to pay for the education of your children, or to buy a home, or to provide for a comfortable retirement. Whatever your financial goals, the dividend-based stock market strategies explained in this book can help you achieve them—slowly and steadily.

Ours is not a "get-rich-quick" approach. We won't show you how to spot hot new trends or buy shares of companies that are just going public. Instead, we'll teach you how to identify long-term (and very profitable) patterns in high-quality stocks.

Nor will we tell you how to time the stock market, because we don't believe it can be done consistently. Attempting to pick the "right" and "wrong" times to own stocks is a fool's errand: The stock market's short-term gyrations are never completely predictable. Instead, we will show you how to pick outstanding stocks that produce steady returns in both good markets and bad.

We won't tell you a thing about bonds, real estate, gold, gems, art works, or anything else people buy and sell in an attempt to make money. True, Old Master paintings sometimes appreciate faster than stocks for long periods of time. But how many people do you know who can afford to buy a Rembrandt? In the seven decades since 1928, no other readily available investment has beaten the gains from common stocks. And that time frame includes the Great Depression as well as the decade-long bear market that ended in 1982.

This book will provide you with the insights, guidelines, and tools you need for a lifetime of profitable stock market investing. We've even included numerous lists of stocks worth considering for your portfolio. But to use this information successfully, you must have both patience and flexibility.

Patience is, by far, more difficult. There will be times (most recently the bull market surge that began in 1995) when the strategies we outline will seem slow, outdated, and even irrelevant. As friends, relatives, and even the occasional cab driver boast of their prowess in picking the latest trendy stock, you will be tempted to abandon the slow-and-steady approach we advocate.

Don't. Hot stocks cool off as investors' perceptions change, and money made quickly can be lost just as rapidly.

Neither do we suggest that you should simply buy stocks from the lists in this book and hold them forever without periodic evaluation. The only constant in life is change: Companies merge, enter new businesses, exit old ones, change managements, and face new competitors every day. While we advocate long-term stock investments, we would never tell you that any stock should be a permanent part of your portfolio. You should always keep up with developments in the companies whose stocks you own. Read their annual and quarterly reports as well as a good daily or weekly summary of business news that will alert you to important developments. When the reasons you bought the stock are no longer valid, you must be flexible enough to sell.

You don't need a lot of money to begin using our strategies. Readers with limited means should consider mutual funds (see Chapter 6) and dividend reinvestment plans (Chapter 5) as ways of making modest regular investments. Also, you won't need a knowledge of higher mathematics to use this book. We've often found that the more complex the equation describing an investment, the more likely you are to lose money on it. A pencil, a note pad, and a pocket calculator are all you'll need to perform any calculation in this book.

Why Dividends Are Important

Dividends are the Rodney Dangerfield of investing: They get no respect. Not many people brag about dividend-paying stocks that they've owned for a dozen years. A regular annual return over a long period of time just doesn't seem to invite the envy of friends and relatives. But in many ways, investing in stocks that pay dividends is like betting on the tortoise in Aesop's fable. Even though the hare is faster, slow and steady wins the race.

We think that dividends, and the slow-and-steady investment philosophy that they suggest, deserve a lot of respect. Dividends are excellent tools for analyzing conservative stock investments. Growing dividends can lead you to shares of companies whose managements are confident about future earnings. Dividend yields can indicate when a stock is undervalued. And filling your portfolio with stocks that pay dividends can cut down on the overall volatility of your investment holdings.

At this point, it might be a good idea to define some of our terms. *Dividends* are the per-share cash payments that many publicly traded companies provide to their shareholders. If a company pays a dividend, you will find its annual cash payment listed in the stock tables of major newspapers under the column heading "DIV."

Some companies pay dividends in additional shares. These are called *stock dividends* in contrast to the more common cash dividends. In this book, we will be discussing dividends paid in cash, unless we indicate otherwise. Most companies pay cash dividends quarterly. But since the board of directors can vote to increase or decrease a company's dividend at any time during the year, investment professionals take the latest quarterly per-share payment and multiply that figure by four to come up with the *indicated dividend,* which is simply what you would expect to receive in payments per share of common stock in the coming year. In common usage, the term *current dividend* also means the indicated dividend. Unless we indicate otherwise, when we discuss historical dividend information in this book, we will use the actual amount paid per share during the year in question.

If a company has announced a dividend increase, that new quarterly figure will be multiplied by four to arrive at the indicated dividend. For example, in late 1997, health care company Abbott Laboratories declared a quarterly dividend of $0.27 a share, payable to its shareholders on February 15, 1998. Newspaper stock listings showed Abbott's dividend as 1.08, which was the indicated rate (four times the quarterly payment of 27 cents) at that time. Before Abbott paid its next shareholder dividend in May 1998, the board had voted to increase the quarterly payment to $0.30 a share. As soon as the announcement was made, newspapers began listing Abbott's dividend as 1.20, the new indicated rate.

When Abbott's board voted to increase the dividend, it also approved a 2-for-1 stock split, effective June 1, 1998. Splits, which are the stock market equivalent of getting two five-dollar bills for a ten, are not reflected in newspaper stock tables until they are effective.

People new to investing often confuse dividend and *yield*. A stock's yield, which is given as a percent, is simply its indicated dividend divided by the current price of a share. Since share prices move up and down in the stock market and change daily for most common stocks, the yield will vary much more than the dividend. Again, let's take Abbott Laboratories as an example. On November 4, 1997, Abbott's stock ended the trading day at $63 a share. Since we know that its indicated dividend on that date was $1.08, the stock's yield was 1.7%. A little more than two months later, Abbott's stock closed at 70. Although the indicated dividend remained the same, the yield had fallen to 1.5%.

An important concept to understand is *total return*, which encompasses an investment's price change plus any income it generates. In the case of stocks, the income is from dividends. The total return from dividend-paying stocks takes on even greater importance in periods of market weakness. In 1994, the stock market ended the year slightly below where it began. Over the course of that year, the shares of personal care and household products maker Colgate-Palmolive outpaced the market by rising only 1.6%. Yet owners of Colgate stock had a total return of 3.3% in 1994, because they received dividends in addition to the increased value of their shares.

Over the last 70 years, the total return of stocks in general, as measured by the S&P 500 index, has been a little less than 11% annually. Dividend-paying stocks can give you a leg up on your main goal in investing: making money. If, for example, you buy a good stock that yields 3%, you're more than a quarter of the way to matching the market's historical performance. That's an important advantage, since most professional money managers fail to outperform the market on a consistent basis. From 1988 through 1997, only 18.4% of diversified equity mutual funds beat the performance of the "500," according to Morningstar, Inc., which tracks mutual fund performance.

As we said, dividends don't get much respect from the average investor. Even though picking stocks with growing dividends or above-average current dividends makes it easier to succeed at building your nest egg, most novice investors, and many professionals, ignore these payments when selecting stocks. They've been misled into thinking that investing doesn't require patience. In a world of instant gratification, many people look for a hot stock to buy today at 7 and sell in three weeks at 20. Unfortunately, such results are more often the stuff of cocktail party chatter than reality. Most investors who try their hands at hot stocks only get burned.

You Can Bank on It

Dividends, on the other hand, are real. They represent a tangible return to you, the shareholder. They are payment to you as an owner of a going business. What's more, you don't have to give up your ownership stake in a company to earn this return. In contrast, unless you want to get involved with options, the only way you can realize a return on shares that don't pay dividends is to sell them.

Dividends are money in the bank. Once you receive the check, or the credit to your brokerage account, that money is yours. It can't be taken away from you. Unrealized capital gains, however, can disappear quickly, sometimes in a single day. In bear markets, you may not even have any gains to lose. Dividends provide your only return when stocks are weak. Figure 1-1 shows the decade immediately preceding the great bull market that began in August 1982. If you had invested $100 in the stock

Figure 1-1. Effect of Dividends in a Flat Market. This chart shows the decade immediately preceding the great bull market that began in August 1982.

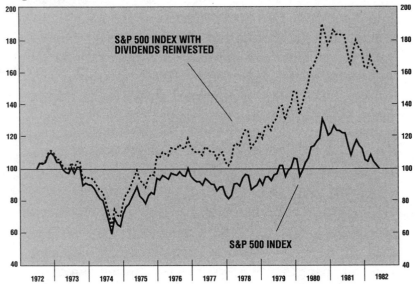

market (as measured by the S&P 500 index) in the summer of 1972, your investment would have been worth about the same *ten years* later. But had you reinvested dividends, the value of your holdings would have been *almost 60% higher.* This is one of the best examples in modern times of the power of dividends to provide returns in a flat market.

As we've mentioned, stocks didn't have a great year in 1994. The S&P 500 index, which professionals use as a proxy for the general market since it represents about 70% of the value of all U.S. common stocks, fell 1.5% for the year. Despite that small decline, an investor who

Figure 1-2. Price Change, Yield, and Total Return of S&P 500 Index. Even in a strong bull market, dividends provide a significant return. In down years, such as 1990 and 1994, they are the *only* return on your stock investments.

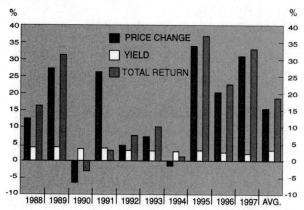

owned an index fund that replicates the "500" still showed a small total return (about 1.3%, not counting the fund's expenses) because of dividend-paying stocks in the index.

The next chart (Fig. 1-2) shows the price change, the annual yield, and the total return of the S&P 500 for each of the ten years ending in 1997. We assumed that you had "bought" the S&P 500 at the start of each year and collected the actual dividends paid on the stocks (in proportion to their weighting in the index) throughout the year. Note the yield of the "500" in relation to its gain or loss in each of the years. In the years 1990 and 1994, the yield from dividends was the only income an investor in the market had. Over the ten-year period, the yield of the "500" averaged 3.1%, while the market posted an average price gain of 15.5%. In other words, cash dividends equaled 20% of the average appreciation of stocks during that period. For the many investors who take dividends in cash, rather than reinvesting them in additional shares of a stock, this is a realistic view. If you do reinvest your dividends, as we'll discuss in Chapter 5, your returns should be greater.

True, your future dividends from common shares aren't guaranteed. Buying stocks is not the same as depositing your savings in a bank backed by federal insurance. In investing, the caveat has always been that past performance is no guarantee of future results. Just because a company has steadily paid or increased its dividend for many years does not mean that it will always do so. In May 1994, FPL Group, a Florida-based electric utility holding company, cut its annual dividend from $2.48 to $1.68 per share, even though it had increased the payment annually for the preceding forty-eight years. The news sent shock waves throughout the investment community, and the company's shares plunged almost 14% on the day of the announcement.

What went unnoticed in all the furor surrounding FPL's dividend cut is how rare such an action really is. The calendar year in which FPL cut its dividend saw fifty-nine companies decrease their dividends and another seventy-seven corporations omit their dividends entirely. Compared to these 136 "unfavorable" dividend actions, there were 1,826 dividend increases reported in 1994. That makes more than thirteen increases for every omitted or decreased dividend.

And although 1994 was a good year for dividends, it was not unique. Since 1956, the average yearly ratio of dividend increases to dividend cuts and omissions has been 8.4 to 1. Only once, in 1958, did cuts and omissions exceed dividend increases.

One reason payments tend to rise rather than fall over time is that most companies that pay dividends are considered mature. While mature may be a compliment in most parts of the world, in investment circles the term often is pejorative. Aggressive investors seek out young, dynamic companies that can grow their earnings at 20%, 30%, or more each year. These companies are still building their businesses and plow back all of their earnings into expanding operations. In contrast, so the theory goes, mature companies can't get a good enough return on further investments in their traditional businesses, so they pay out a large part of their profits to shareholders in the form of dividends.

Of course, reality clashes with this overly simplified division between growing companies and mature ones. General Electric is on almost everyone's list of dynamic, growing companies. The diversified giant operates in twelve major business lines and is an industry leader in most of them. Its products range from high-tech jet aircraft engines to mundane light bulbs (see Chapter 9). In the ten years ended 1997, GE posted a compound annual per-share earnings gain of 12%. Not bad for a company that has paid a dividend since 1899 and increased it every year since 1975. And General Electric is far from alone. As we'll show you in the chapters that follow, you don't have to invest in has-been companies to benefit from a strategy that emphasizes dividend growth.

Dividends Provide Stability

For as long as anyone can remember, investors have intuitively understood that dividend-paying stocks provide a higher degree of price stability than non-dividend-paying issues. When the market declines, as it does periodically (some 29% of the time since the New York Stock Exchange was founded in 1792), most stocks will drop in value. In these corrections, investors tend to hold on to stocks that will provide them with another cash payment in a few months and dump those whose only attraction is that they are expected to go up in price. In other words, stocks that pay dividends have less volatility than those that don't. The flip side of this statement is that in strong bull markets, stocks that pay dividends are not the highest fliers. But remember, the tortoise, over time, beats the hare!

The protective aspects of dividend-paying stocks were apparent in the October 19, 1987 stock market crash. In the space of that one day, the widely followed Dow Jones Industrial Average (composed of thirty major blue chip stocks) fell 508 points, or 22.6%. That surpassed the infamous October 1929 crash, in which the Dow fell 12.8% in a day, to become the largest one-day decline in the history of the modern stock market.

A major academic study of the October 1987 event showed that stocks with the highest yields prior to the crash fell 21.2%, while stocks that paid no dividends tumbled 32%. Dr. Avner Arvel, professor of finance at Cornell University, and his colleagues Steven Carvell and Erik Postnieks, studied the price action of 2,000 stocks in the 1987 crash and reported their results in the May/June 1988 issue of *Harvard Business Review*. The stocks in their study included issues listed on the New York Stock Exchange and the American Stock Exchange or traded in the Nasdaq over-the-counter market, and the authors looked at these issues from several perspectives, including dividend yield.

Admittedly, a drop of "only" 21% in a single day is nothing to cheer about. But consider two hypothetical portfolios, one containing the top dividend payers and the other the non-payers. Each portfolio is worth $10,000 prior to the 1987 crash. Following the drop, the dividend-paying portfolio would have been worth $1,080 more than the portfolio that didn't pay dividends. As Dr. Arvel and his colleagues noted, "When the market environment is very uncertain, a bird in the hand is worth more than two in the bush."

This study of the 1987 crash also divided the 2,000-stock sample by industry group. It should not come as a surprise that the best-performing industry group during the crash was electric utilities. Those stocks, usually among the highest-yielding common stocks in the market, fell only 10.5%.

The Tax Question

Investment advisors who favor stocks that don't pay dividends usually like to bring up the subject of taxes. They note with some glee that, under the most recent revision of the tax code, capital gains are taxed at a maximum of 20%, while dividends are treated as ordinary income.

This is true, but the percentage figures alone don't give you a full picture of how much you pay in taxes on dividends vs. capital gains. Although the rate is higher on dividends, the dollar amount in taxes is usually much lower and paid over a period of years. In contrast, taxes on capital gains that were years in the making are due all at once.

Let's say you bought 100 shares of Merck & Co., a leading pharmaceutical maker, at the end of 1992. If you had purchased the shares at their closing price on December 31, you would have paid $4,337.50 (not counting brokerage commissions) for your position. Merck paid $1.06 a share in dividends in 1993 and increased its payments to shareholders every year. In the five years ended 1997, you would have collected $672 in dividends on your 100 shares of Merck.

For the sake of simplicity, we'll assume that current tax rates were in effect for the entire five-year period. If you were in the 28% marginal tax bracket (Internal Revenue Service figures indicate that more than 90% of individual filers pay a marginal rate of 28% or less), your tax liability on Merck's dividend payments would have amounted to $188.16 *over five years.* What's more, the most you would have paid in any one year was $48.72. If you had sold your Merck shares at their closing price of $106 on the last day of 1997, you would have realized a capital gain of $6,262.50 ($10,600 − $4,337.50, not counting commissions). And you would have owed 20%, or $1,252.50 in capital gains taxes *all at once.*

As the above example shows, what you pay in taxes is more important than the marginal tax rate. But we can already hear objections to our example. After all, Merck is a growth stock. True, but one that pays a dividend and regularly increases it, which is the kind of stock we think you should own.

Nevertheless, in deference to dividend-phobic investors, we'll do the same exercise with a higher-yielding stock. At the end of 1992, Southern Co. provided a 5.7% yield. If you had purchased 100 shares of this power company at their closing price on December 31, you would have paid $3,850 (excluding commission) for your position. Southern paid $2.28 a share in dividends in 1993. Like Merck, the company increased its dividend in each of the five years in question. If you had owned Southern stock for that period, you would have collected $1,220 in dividends.

At the 28% marginal tax bracket, your taxes on Southern's dividends would have come to $341.60 *over five years.* The most you would have paid in any single year was $72.80. In 1994, Southern shares split 2-for-1. As a result, you would have sold 200 shares, worth a total of $5,175, at the end of 1997. You would have realized a capital gain of $1,325 ($5,175 – $3,850, not counting commission). And while your 20% tax on that gain ($265) is less than the $341.60 you would have paid in taxes on your dividends over five years, it would have been due all at once. In fact, your capital gains liability would have been 3.6 times the highest amount you would have paid in any year on your dividend income from Southern's stock.

For the vast majority of investors, a dollar of dividend income costs only eight cents more in taxes than a dollar of capital gains. But what if you are in the 36% or even the top 39.6% bracket? Paying more in taxes is never fun, but you should not eliminate dividend payers from your investment portfolio. Remember, a dividend paid to you is real; capital gains remain potential until you sell the shares. Also, as we have noted, these more conservative dividend-paying issues can provide needed stability to your assets. They also make excellent choices for self-directed tax-deferred retirement accounts. More on that in Chapter 5.

Summing Up

1. *A good dividend-paying stock will give you a leg up on your investment goals.*

2. *Dividends allow you to realize a return on your stock investment without giving up ownership.*

3. *Once paid, the dividend is yours to keep.*

4. *Although dividends are not guaranteed, far more companies raise payments than cut them.*

5. *Dividend-paying stocks provide greater stability in market downturns.*

6. *While dividend income (and the taxes on it) are spread out, capital gains taxes are due all at once.*

7. *For most investors, a dollar of dividend income costs only eight cents more in taxes than a dollar of capital gains.*

What to Look for in a Dividend-Paying Stock

The novice investor looking for an income stock often starts and ends the search by seeking out the highest-yielding stocks. Wrong! Heed the hoary advice: If it looks too good to be true, it probably is.

A stock with a mouthwatering yield may well be under water in a matter of months. Never buy a stock on the basis of yield alone. A well-above-average yield means that the stock price is depressed either because earnings have been disappointing or there's some adverse news about to be announced. The high yield thus could signal either a dividend cut or dividend omission somewhere down the line.

Examples abound: IBM yielded a lofty 10% (vs. a 2.9% yield on the S&P 500 index) in January 1993, less than a month before the company announced a 55% cut in the dividend. In the late 1980s, many banks also sported juicy yields just before the real estate market crashed and they were forced to write off sizable loans. These writeoffs resulted in declining profits and wholesale dividend reductions or omissions.

Electric utilities, too, were returning extremely high yields in the mid-1980s when many of their nuclear plants were in trouble. Following the infamous Three Mile Island nuclear plant accident in early 1979, the federal Nuclear Regulatory Commission became a more vigilant watchdog, mandating expensive safety measures for nuclear plant construction. That led to huge cost overruns on the plants, while at the same time, electricity demand was falling due mainly to conservation efforts. Plant cancellations became the order of the day, which depressed earnings and resulted in widespread unfavorable dividend actions.

More recently, Capstead Mortgage, a real estate investment trust (REIT) specializing in mortgages, yielded more than 12% in early February 1998, compared with a then more typical 8% for a mortgage REIT issue. On March 9, Capstead announced a 19% cut in the annual dividend to $2.00 from $2.46. The company, which funds long-term investments with short-term money, was being hurt by a flat yield curve (long-term interest rates about equal to short-term rates). In mid-June, Capstead shares had fallen to where they were yielding more than 14%, well above the yield of the typical mortgage REIT, which suggested that another dividend cut could be in the works. In fact, a few weeks later, the company announced that it would further slash the dividend, and the stock fell sharply. Subsequently, Capstead eliminated the dividend.

How to Avoid Clinkers

To avoid situations like those cited above, your first step should be to check the yields of stocks in the same industry as the issue you're thinking of buying. You can do this by consulting *Standard & Poor's Analysts' Handbook Monthly Supplement,* found in many libraries, which contains dividend yields of all industry groups. *The Value Line Investment Survey* is also a good source to research yields. If you find that the industry average yield is considerably lower than that of your buy candidate, steer clear, unless you're willing to take on above-average risk. We'll discuss when to break this rule in Chapter 8.

You will actually fare better by buying lower-yielding stocks that have a long history of boosting dividends each year. Although such companies typically don't declare large increases, when dividend payments are hiked regularly, the yield on your original investment can climb dramatically over time.

Take General Electric, as an example. If you had bought the stock of this diversified company (aircraft engines, medical and power systems, appliances, broadcasting and financial services) in 1988 at a median price of $11 (adjusted for stock splits), you would have received a dividend of $0.36 for a yield of less than 3.3%. Based on the 1998 indicated dividend rate of $1.20, however, you would be getting a return of 10.9% on your 1988 cost. In addition, through mid-1998 the shares appreciated 682%. We'll have more to say on this strategy in Chapter 3.

Table 2-1 lists companies that have increased their dividends in each of the ten years from 1988 to 1997. Each of the stocks has outpaced by a wide margin the 59% increase in dividends posted by the benchmark S&P 500 index over the last decade. In addition, each of the stocks more than doubled dividend payments during the same 10 years. Top honors go to Paychex, Inc. (a provider of computerized payroll accounting services), which paid $0.01 annually in 1988 (adjusted for splits) and $0.18 ten years later, for a gain of more than 2,000%.

Although past increases can't be projected into the future, investors looking for income can use the list to pick stocks that have a strong history of dividend boosts and are therefore likely to continue. Some of those companies have paid dividends for a long stretch of time. Table 2-2 lists companies that have paid dividends for 69 years or longer.

Payout Ratios

After you've determined that a stock's yield is not out of whack, take a look at the payout ratio. An important indicator of a company's ability to sustain good dividend growth, the payout ratio is simply the dividend expressed as a percentage of earnings, usually projected current-year profits. The Institutional Brokers Estimate System, known on Wall Street as I/B/E/S (pronounced "eye-bess") carries consensus earnings estimates for more than 5,000 U.S. and

Table 2-1. Dividend Increase Champions

Company	Ticker	Industry	10-year Div. Increase %
Paychex, Inc.	PAYX	Financial Services	2005.3
Schwab (Chas.) Corp.	SCH	Financial Services	1718.2
Home Depot	HD	Retail	1134.6
MYR Group	MYR	Manufacturing	937.0
Travelers Group	TRV	Financial Services	935.2
Argonaut Group	AGII	Financial Services	884.4
Federal Nat'l Mtge.	FNM	Financial Services	793.0
Sysco Corp.	SYY	Food Distribution	679.2
First Bancorp (NC)	FBNC	Financial Services	575.7
Mercury General	MCY	Financial Services	559.1
Washington Mutual	WAMU	Financial Services	552.8
T.Rowe Price Assoc.	TROW	Financial Services	547.6
Cintas Corp.	CTAS	Uniforms	536.0
Hewlett-Packard	HWP	Computer Manufacturing	522.2
Archer-Daniels-Midland	ADM	Food Processing	517.3
Jones Pharma	JMED	Health Care	506.1
Wal-Mart Stores	WMT	Retail	505.5
Virco Mfg.	VIR	Furniture	488.2
Brady Corp.	BRCOA	Adhesives	480.8
Fluor Corp.	FLR	Engineering	471.4
Hawkins Chemical	HWKN	Chemicals	452.5
ASA Holdings	ASAI	Transportation	450.0
Disney (Walt) Co.	DIS	Leisure	447.8
CORUS Bankshares	CORS	Financial Services	440.0
Charter One Fin'l	COFI	Financial Services	417.1
MBIA Inc.	MBI	Financial Services	403.2
United Asset Mgmt.	UAM	Financial Services	400.0
Reuters Group ADS	RTRSY	Media	391.4
Hasbro Inc.	HAS	Toys	380.5

Table 2-1. Dividend Increase Champions *(continued)*

Company	Ticker	Industry	10-year Div. Increase %
SLM Holding	SLM	Financial Services	378.2
MASSBANK Corp	MASB	Financial Services	376.2
Cohu Inc.	COHU	Electronics	374.1
McClatchy Co. 'A'	MNI	Publishing	370.6
Eaton Vance	EV	Financial Services	368.3
Synovus Financial	SNV	Financial Services	364.1
BankAmerica Corp.	BAC	Financial Services	360.0
Nucor Corp.	NUE	Steel	346.5
Cooper Tire & Rubber	CTB	Tires	340.8
Watts Industries 'A'	WTS	Manufacturing	337.5
Gillette Co.	G	Personal Care	336.5
FNB Corp. (PA)	FBAN	Financial Services	336.4
Culp Inc.	CFI	Furniture	326.8
UNUM Corp.	UNM	Financial Services	314.0
Fidelity National Fin'l	FNF	Financial Services	312.6
Franklin Resources	BEN	Financial Services	309.8
Fifth Third Bancorp	FITB	Financial Services	300.3
Omnicare, Inc.	OCR	Health Care	300.0
ALLIED Group	GRP	Financial Services	299.1
Federal Signal	FSS	Manufacturing	294.0
Pall Corp.	PLL	Manufacturing	287.5
Valspar Corp.	VAL	Chemicals	281.8
Superior Indus. Int'l	SUP	Auto Parts	279.4
Reynolds & Reynolds	REY	Information Systems	278.9
Automatic Data Processing	AUD	Computer Services	278.6
McCormick & Co.	MCCRK	Food	276.5

Company	Ticker	Industry	10-year Div. Increase %
Alliance Capital Mgmt.	AC	Financial Services	275.8
Brenton Banks	BRBK	Financial Services	274.0
Tootsie Roll Indus.	TR	Food	270.7
Albertson's, Inc.	ABS	Retail (Supermarkets)	267.6
Campbell Soup	CPB	Food	265.2
Westamerica Bancorporation	WABC	Financial Services	260.1
Baldor Electric	BEZ	Electrical Equipment	257.5
Abbott Laboratories	ABT	Health Care	255.6
Illinois Tool Works	ITW	Manufacturing	255.6
Harleysville Savings Bank	HARL	Financial Services	254.8
ConAgra Inc.	CAG	Food	253.5
Analysts Int'l	ANLY	Computer Services	253.2
Coca-Cola Co.	KO	Beverages	252.9
Raven Indus.	RAVN	Manufacturing	252.9
Norwest Corp.	NOB	Financial Services	247.4
Pitney Bowes	PBI	Office Equipment	246.2
Schering-Plough	SGP	Health Care	242.7
Great Lakes Chemical	GLK	Chemicals	236.8
Glacier Bancorp	GBCI	Financial Services	235.2
First Source Corp.	SRCE	Financial Services	234.4
Golden West Fin'l	GDW	Financial Services	233.3
Hannaford Bros.	HRD	Retail (Supermarkets)	233.3
Superior Surgical	SGC	Textiles (Apparel)	233.3
Nat'l Penn Bancshares	NPBC	Financial Services	231.7
State Street Corp.	STT	Financial Services	231.0

Table 2-1. Dividend Increase Champions *(continued)*

Company	Ticker	Industry	10-year Div. Increase %
Merck & Co.	MRK	Health Care	229.3
Associated Banc-Corp.	ASBC	Financial Services	229.0
PepsiCo Inc.	PEP	Beverages	226.2
Schulman (A.)	SHLM	Chemicals	223.5
BB&T Corp.	BBK	Financial Services	220.7
Tompkins County Trustco	TMP	Financial Services	220.1
Star Banc Corp.	STB	Financial Services	219.1
Johnson & Johnson	JNJ	Health Care	214.3
Compass Bancshares	CBSS	Financial Services	214.0
Avery Dennison Corp.	AVY	Manufacturing	211.1
Family Dollar Stores	FDO	Retail	208.7
Shoreline Financial	SLFC	Financial Services	208.5
Firstar Corp	FSR	Financial Services	208.3
Banc One Corp.	ONE	Financial Services	203.0
Huntington Bancshares	HBAN	Financial Services	202.8
Synalloy Corp.	SYNC	Metal Fabricators	200.1
Warner-Lambert	WLA	Health Care	200.0
Wallace Computer Svc.	WCS	Office Equipment	198.8
AFLAC Inc.	AFL	Financial Services	197.5
Jefferson-Pilot	JP	Financial Services	197.2
First Union Corp.	FTU	Financial Services	196.0
Cincinnati Financial	CINF	Financial Services	195.4
Crawford & Co.	CRD.B	Financial Services	194.1
Bemis Co.	BMS	Containers	193.3

Company	Ticker	Industry	10-year Div. Increase %
General Electric	GE	Electrical Equipment	192.7
Hormel Foods	HRL	Food	190.9
American Stores	ASC	Retail (Supermarkets)	188.0
Hillenbrand Industries	HB	Burial Caskets	188.0
American Int'l Group	AIG	Financial Services	187.9
Tuscarora Inc.	TUSC	Packaging	187.2
First Tenn. National	FTEN	Financial Services	182.9
Colgate-Palmolive	CL	Household Products	182.1
Walgreen Co.	WAG	Retail (Drugstores)	181.8
City Holding	CHCO	Financial Services	178.7
Rubbermaid, Inc.	RBD	Housewares	178.3
Berkley (W.R.)	BKLY	Financial Services	177.0
Suffolk Bancorp	SUBK	Financial Services	176.9
Pfizer, Inc.	PFE	Health Care	176.4

Canadian companies. Your stockbroker should have access to I/B/E/S or a competing estimate service. (See Appendix A for other information sources.) Stocks with a low payout ratio, say below 50%, have more room to increase their dividends. The payout ratio can also serve as a good gauge of growth stocks. Any issue that has increased its dividend by several hundred percent over a decade and still has a payout ratio under 50% has demonstrated strong earnings progress.

Cash Flow

Another helpful tool to determine whether a company's dividend is safe is cash flow. That's simply the company's net

Table 2-2. Long-term Dividend Payers. There are no guarantees in investing, but we assume that most of these companies will continue to pay dividends.

Company	Ticker	Industry	Dividend Paid Since
BankBoston Corp.	BKB	Financial Services	1784
Bank of New York	BK	Financial Services	1785
Fleet Financial Group	FLT	Financial Services	1791
Westpac Banking	WBK	Financial Services	1817
Chase Manhattan	CMB	Financial Services	1827
Bank of Montreal	BMO	Financial Services	1829
Bank of Nova Scotia	BNS*	Financial Services	1834
Providence Energy	PVY	Utilities	1849
Connecticut Energy	CNE	Utilities	1850
CTG Resources	CTG	Utilities	1851
Washington Gas Light	WGL	Utilities	1852
Bay State Gas	BGC	Utilities	1853
ClNergy Corp	CIN	Utilities	1853
U.S. Trust	USTC	Financial Services	1854
Toronto-Dominion Bank	TD	Financial Services	1857
Berkshire Gas	BGAS	Utilities	1858
Star Banc Corp.	STB	Utilities	1863
CT Fin'l Services	CFS*	Financial Services	1865
PNC Bank Corp.	PNC	Financial Services	1865
CIGNA Corp.	Cl	Financial Services	1867
American Express	AXP	Financial Services	1870
Crestar Financial	CF	Financial Services	1870
Royal Bank Canada	RY	Financial Services	1870
HSB Group	HSB	Financial Services	1871
Laurentian Bank, Canada	LB*	Financial Services	1871

Company	Ticker	Industry	Dividend Paid Since
St. Paul Cos.	SPC	Financial Services	1872
Stanley Works	SWK	Tools	1877
Cincinnati Bell	CSN	Telephone	1879
Fall River Gas	FAL	Utilities	1880
AT&T Corp.	T	Telephone	1881
BCE Inc.	BCE	Telephone	1881
Corning Inc.	GLW	Glass	1881
E'town Corp.	ETW	Utilities	1881
Exxon Corp.	XON	Oil/Gas	1882
Carter-Wallace	CAR	Health Care	1883
Consolidated Edison	ED	Utilities	1885
Lilly (Eli)	LLY	Health Care	1885
UGI Corp.	UGI	Utilities	1885
United Water Resources	UWR	Utilities	1886
AlliedSignal Inc.	ALD	Aerospace/Automotive	1887
Aquarion Co.	WTR	Utilities	1890
BCE Energy	BSE	Utilities	1890
Canadian Imperial Bank	BCM	Financial Services	1890
Unicom Corp. UCM	UCM	Utilities	1890
Imperial Oil Ltd.	IMO	Oil/Gas	1891
Procter & Gamble	PG	Household Products	1891
Southern New Eng. Telecom.	SNG	Telephone	1891
Morgan (J.P.)	JPM	Financial Services	1892
Times Mirror 'A'	TMC	Publishing	1892
Westvaco Corp.	W	Forest Products	1892
Coca-Cola Co.	KO	Beverages	1893
Amoco Corp.	AN	Oil/Gas	1894
First Merchants Corp.	FRME	Financial Services	1894
Colgate-Palmolive	CL	Household Products	1895

Table 2-2. Long-term Dividend Payers *(continued)*

Company	Ticker	Industry	Dividend Paid Since
First Tenn Nat'l	FTEN	Financial Services	1895
Mellon Bank Corp.	MEL	Financial Services	1895
Northern Trust	NTRS	Financial Services	1896
General Mills	GIS	Food/Beverages	1898
Shell Transp./Trading	SC	Oil/Gas	1898
Springs Industries 'A'	SMI	Textiles	1898
General Electric	GE	Diversified Mfg.	1899
PPG Industries	PPG	Chemicals	1899
Pacific Century Fin'l	BOH	Financial Services	1899
Washington Water Power	WWP	Utilities	1899
Bristol-Myers Squibb	BMY	Health Care	1900
TECO Energy	TE	Utilities	1900
Union Pacific	UNP	Transportation	1900
United Illuminating	UIL	Utilities	1900
Church & Dwight	CHD	Household Products	1901
Hawaiian Electric Industries	HE	Utilities	1901
Johnson Controls	JCI	Automated Controls	1901
Norfolk Southern	NSC	Transportation	1901
Pfizer, Inc.	PFE	Health Care	1901
Alexander & Baldwin	ALEX	Transportation	1902
Campbell Soup	CPB	Food	1902
Chubb Corp.	CB	Financial Services	1902
Eastman Kodak	EK	Photgraphy	1902
Mobil Corp.	MOB	Oil/Gas	1902
PECO Energy	PE	Utilities	1902
Tribune Co.	TRB	Publishing	1902
Alcatel	ALA	Telecom. Equip.	1903
Central Hudson Gas & Electric	CNH	Utilities	1903

Company	Ticker	Industry	Dividend Paid Since
National Fuel Gas	NFG	Utilities	1903
NationsBank Corp.	NB	Financial Services	1903
Texaco Inc.	TX	Oil/Gas	1903
Bankers Trust NY	BT	Financial Services	1904
duPont (EI) deNemours	DD	Chemicals	1904
Potomac Electric Power	POM	Utilities	1904
Sun Co.	SUN	Oil/Gas	1904
Wiley (John) & Sons	JW.B	Publishing	1904
Fortune Brands	FO	Housewares	1905
Handy & Harman	HNH	Metals	1905
Ameren Corp.	AEE	Utilities	1906
Dow Jones & Co.	DJ	Publishing	1906
Gillette Co.	G	Toiletries	1906
Quaker Oats	OAT	Food	1906
Carpenter Technology	CRS	Steel	1907
Kansas City Life Ins.	KCLI	Financial Services	1907
Public Service Enterprises	PEG	Utilities	1907
Houghton Mifflin	HTN	Publishing	1908
OGE Energy	OGE	Utilities	1908
Orange/Rockland Utilities	ORU	Utilities	1908
UNITIL Corp.	UTL	Utilities	1908
Amer. Electric Power	AEP	Utilities	1909
CalMat Co.	CZM	Concrete	1909
DTE Energy	DTE	Utilities	1909
Edison International	EIX	Utilities	1909
First American Fin'l	FAF	Financial Services	1909

Table 2-2. Long-term Dividend Payers *(continued)*

Company	Ticker	Industry	Dividend Paid Since
Madison Gas & Electric	MDSN	Utilities	1909
Mercantile Bancorp	MTL	Financial Services	1909
Mercantile Bankshares	MRBK	Financial Services	1909
Baltimore Gas & Electric	BGE	Utilities	1910
Ingersoll-Rand	IR	Machinery	1910
Energy East	NEG	Utilities	1910
Northern States Power	NSP	Utilities	1910
State Street Corp.	STT	Financial Services	1910
Donnelley (RR) & Sons	DNY	Printing	1911
Dow Chemical	DOW	Chemicals	1911
Heinz (H.J.)	HNZ	Food	1911
May Dept. Stores	MAY	Retail	1911
Chevron Corp.	CHV	Oil/Gas	1912
Huntington Bancshares	HBAN	Financial Services	1912
Imasco Ltd.	IMS*	Tobacco/Food	1912
Middlesex Water	MSEX	Utilities	1912
UST Inc.	UST	Tobacco	1912
Courtaulds, plc	COU	Chemicals	1913
DQE	DQE	Utilities	1913
Equifax Inc.	EFX	Information Svcs.	1913
Hercules, Inc.	HPC	Chemicals	1913
Jefferson-Pilot	JP	Financial Services	1913
LG & E Energy	LGE	Utilities	1913
Monarch Mach. Tool	MMO	Machinery	1913
Wrigley (Wm.) Jr.	WWY	Chewing Gum	1913
Caterpillar Inc.	CAT	Equipment	1914

Company	Ticker	Industry	Dividend Paid Since
First Union Corp.	FTU	Financial Services	1914
Wilmington Trust Corp.	WILM	Financial Services	1914
Essex County Gas	ECGC	Utilities	1915
General Motors	GM	Automobile	1915
Lincoln Electric	LECO	Industrial Products	1915
Tasty Baking	TBC	Food	1915
CVS Corp.	CVS	Retail (Drugs)	1916
Int'l Bus. Machines	IBM	Computers	1916
Minnesota Mining & Mfg.	MMM	Diversified	1916
Sierra Pacific Resources	SRP	Utilities	1916
Unocal Corp.	UCL	Oil/Gas	1916
British Petroleum	BP	Oil/Gas	1917
Idaho Power	IDA	Utilities	1917
Texas Utilities	TXU	Utilities	1917
Mine Safety Appliances	MNES	Equipment	1918
Pulitzer Publishing	PTZ	Publishing	1918
Union Carbide	UK	Chemicals	1918
American Home Products	AHP	Health Care	1919
Avon Products	AVP	Personal Products	1919
Courier Corp.	CRRC	Publishing	1919
DPL Inc.	DPL	Utilities	1919
GATX Corp.	GMT	Diversified	1919
PG&E Corp.	PCG	Utilities	1919
Bestfoods	BFO	Food	1920
Lincoln National Corp.	LNC	Financial Services	1920
National Westminster	NW	Financial Services	1920
CILCORP, Inc.	CER	Utilities	1921

Table 2-2. Long-term Dividend Payers *(continued)*

Company	Ticker	Industry	Dividend Paid Since
CLARCOR Inc.	CLC	Filtration Services	1921
Deluxe Corp.	DLX	Printing	1921
Kansas City Power & Lt.	KLT	Utilities	1921
Amerada Hess	AHC	Oil/Gas	1922
Bemis Co.	BMS	Packaging	1922
CSX Corp.	CSX	Transportation	1922
Houston Industries	HOU	Utilities	1922
Penney (J.C.)	JCP	Retail	1922
Scripps (E.W.) 'A'	SSP	Publishing	1922
Timken Co.	TKR	Manufacturing	1922
American Nat'l Insurance	ANAT	Financial Services	1923
Brown Group	BG	Shoes	1923
Cincinnati Milacron	CMZ	Machinery	1923
Eaton Corp.	ETN	Auto Parts	1923
Int'l Multifoods	IMC	Food	1923
Kellogg Co.	K	Food	1923
Marsh & McLennan	MMC	Financial Services	1923
Media General Cl. 'A'	MEG.A	Publishing	1923
NUI Corp.	NUI	Utilities	1923
Ohio Casualty	OCAS	Financial Services	1923
Popular Inc.	BPOP	Financial Services	1923
Lab Holdings	LABH	Health Care	1924
Western Resources	WR	Utilities	1924
Arvin Industries	ARV	Auto Parts	1925
Bangor Hydro Electric	BGR	Utilities	1925
Dominion Resources	D	Utilities	1925
Monsanto Co.	MTC	Chemicals	1925
Pennzoil Co.	PZL	Oil/Gas	1925
Provident Companies	PVT	Financial Services	1925

Company	Ticker	Industry	Dividend Paid Since
Sonoco Products	SON	Packaging	1925
Cordant Technologies	CCD	Aerospace	1925
Waverly Inc.	WAVR	Publishing	1925
Abbott Laboratories	ABT	Health Care	1926
Becton, Dickinson	BDX	Health Care	1926
Duke Energy	DUK	Utilities	1926
Frontier Corp.	FRO	Telephone	1926
Greif Bros Cl. 'A'	GBCOA	Containers	1926
Household Int'l	HI	Financial Services	1926
Nash Finch Co.	NAFC	Retail	1926
Olin Corp.	OLN	Chemicals	1926
Owens & Minor	OMI	Health Care	1926
Protective Life Corp.	PL	Financial Services	1926
Warner-Lambert	WLA	Health Care	1926
Archer-Daniels-Midland	ADM	Agribusiness	1927
Atlantic Richfield	ARC	Oil/Gas	1927
Banta Corp.	BNTA	Packaging	1927
Fleming Cos.	FLM	Distribution	1927
Georgia-Pacific	GP	Forest Products	1927
Imperial Chemical	ICI	Chemicals	1927
Northeast Utilities	NU	Utilities	1927
Rohm & Haas	ROH	Chemicals	1927
Standard Register	SR	Business Forms	1927
Universal Corp.	UVV	Tobacco	1927
British American Tobacco	BTI	Tobacco	1928
Eastern Utilities Assoc.	EUA	Utilities	1928
Honeywell, Inc.	HON	Automated Controls	1928
HormelFoods	HRL	Food	1928
Nalco Chemical	NLC	Chemicals	1928
Philip Morris Cos.	MO	Tobacco	1928

Table 2-2. Long-term Dividend Payers *(continued)*

Company	Ticker	Industry	Dividend Paid Since
American General	AGC	Financial Services	1929
Briggs & Stratton	BGG	Engines	1929
First Hawaiian	FHWN	Financial Services	1929
Gannett Co.	GCI	Publishing	1929
McCormick & Co.	MCCRK	Food	1929
Whirlpool Corp.	WHR	Appliances	1929

*Trades on Toronto Exchange.

income plus depreciation and amortization. Statements of cash flow can be found after the balance sheet, toward the back of annual reports. A rule of thumb is that cash flow should be at least three times the dividend payout. Financial companies, such as banks, are the exception, since nearly all of their assets are cash. (For guidelines regarding banks see the section on Traditional Income Stocks following.)

Quality Rankings

As a quick test for a reliable income stock, you can check the quality ranking awarded by Standard & Poor's. The quality ranking measures the growth and stability of a company's earnings and dividends over the past ten years. A+ is highest; A, high; A–, above average; B+, average; B, below average; B–, low; C, lowest; D, in reorganization; NR, not ranked. Quality rankings are not intended to predict stock price movements. The rankings are listed in *Standard & Poor's Stock Guide*, which can be found in the business section of many libraries. Value Line's relative safety rankings are also a good guide: 1 (highest) and 2 (above average).

Basics Worth Checking

As with any stock you are considering, you should check a dividend-paying equity's price-earnings ratio (P/E) against the P/E ratios of others in its industry. The P/E ratio is the most widely used tool for evaluating stocks since it quickly shows how much investors are willing to pay for each dollar of a company's earnings. Be sure you are comparing apples to apples: Some investors calculate P/E ratios using earnings of the most recent twelve months; others use estimated earnings.

P/Es generally are higher when inflation and interest rates are low. That's because low inflation means profits are the result of underlying business conditions and not simply the result of rising selling prices. A stock that sports a P/E ratio much higher than those of its competitors demands closer inspection. A high P/E (based on trailing profits) could indicate that the company has had recent earnings problems. When it's calculated on estimated earnings, a high P/E might mean that investors are bidding up the shares because of the company's strong growth prospects. Or a high P/E could simply mean a stock is temporarily overvalued. Check the stock's P/E range over the last five years to help you evaluate it.

While lower-than-average P/E multiples can signal attractive buys, they don't always. Cyclical stocks (those whose fortunes are more closely tied to economic cycles, such as chemicals and steel) often sell at low P/E multiples when investors believe that their peak profits for a given cycle are near.

Traditional Income Stocks

Electric and gas utilities, banks, and real estate investment trusts (REITs) are higher-yielding stocks that are attractive for income investors. You should keep in mind that all of these groups are sensitive to interest rates.

High interest rates cut into the profits of the utilities, since they need a large amount of capital to run operations and thus borrow heavily. Banks suffer in a high interest rate environment because of a narrowing of their net interest margins (the spread between the cost of funds and the rate charged for loans). Margins can be squeezed because of the lag between the time that rates on deposits increase and the time that various assets, including loans, are repriced. Also, high interest rates reduce the value of a bank's fixed-rate (bond) portfolio. When interest rates rise, older bonds fall in price so that their yields move up to match the higher yield of new bonds. Conversely, when interest rates fall, older bonds rise in value. As a result, when rates climb, banks have to reposition their portfolios to account for the reduced valuations and often incur charges against profits.

REITs' earnings are affected by high rates because their borrowing costs for property purchases increase. At the same time, REIT issues are regarded as bond substitutes, or yield plays. Since bonds trade primarily based on interest rate movements, REIT stocks do also. When interest rates rise, REITs, like bonds, generally drop in value, and when rates decline, the stocks typically advance. All of these groups, in fact, compete with fixed-income investments.

Following is an overview of traditional income groups. We'll tell you what to look for in each industry to assure you're picking the right stocks.

Electric Utilities

Stocks of electric utilities have been perhaps the number one haven for equity investors seeking income. The group pays out a large part of its earnings in dividends, and a good many of the companies' profits and cash flow are healthy enough to support yearly dividend hikes—increases that, in some cases, have managed to keep up with inflation over time.

As with any industry, however, selectivity is always in order. As mentioned earlier, earnings and dividends of many of the utilities in the mid-1980s were adversely affected by nuclear generating plant problems. More recently, investors have been concerned over increasing industry competition and greater environmental regulations.

The Energy Policy Act of 1992 promotes competition in the electric generation market and mandates wholesale transmission access. A utility may soon be required to allow its transmission facilities to be used for transactions between any power-generating entity and another utility, which, in turn, would sell the power to the end-user.

Competition, especially for industrial and commercial customers, is heating up. Discounts to large industrial customers have already been seen, and utilities have been merging in order to survive in the new environment. One of the most important merger proposals was announced in December 1997, when American Electric Power agreed to acquire Central and South West in a stock-for-stock transaction valued at $6.6 billion. The combination would result in the largest electric utility in the U.S., serving six million customers in 11 states. Although a similarly large merger proposal between Northern States Power and Wisconsin Energy was not approved by the Federal Energy Regulatory Commission on anticompetitive grounds, the American Electric Power-Central and South West combination is expected to get the green light because the merger would not increase the combined companies' market power within any state in which they do business. The merger should be completed some time in 1999.

Utilities are also acquiring foreign companies. In May 1998, for example, Texas Utilities purchased the U.K.-based The Eastern Group (formerly The Energy Group). U.S. utilities in mid-1998 owned eight of the 12 regional electric companies in the U.K.

With profits hard won, utilities have had to shutter inefficient facilities, cut staff, and reduce dividends. Over the last ten years, more than two dozen electric utilities have slashed dividend payments.

In selecting electric utilities, look for: (1) an S&P quality ranking of at least B+; (2) companies whose five-year dividend growth rate has exceeded the inflation rate;

and (3) a relatively modest payout ratio (dividends as a percentage of estimated current-year profits). Utilities pay out a much larger portion of their profits than other industries, but a payout ratio above 80% should set off an alarm.

Gas Utilities

Government policies to clean up the environment have brightened prospects for natural gas stocks. Natural gas is a clean-burning fuel, and demand over at least the next few years should be above the historical norm. Some natural gas distributors are expected to enhance their earnings potential by expanding into nontraditional markets, such as cogeneration, combined-cycle power generation, and natural gas vehicles.

The new markets have been spurred by the National Energy Policy Act of 1992 and the Clean Air Act amendments passed in 1990, which encourage the use of natural gas because of the abundance of U.S. supplies and the fuel's environmental advantage. Of the new markets, power generation offers the greatest boost to overall gas demand. Power generators such as electric utilities probably will displace some usage of coal and oil with natural gas. Even without the demand stimulus associated with recent legislation, gas demand growth in this market would be significant.

More and more natural gas companies are being acquired by electric utilities. In 1997, Duke Power, one of the nation's largest electric utilities, acquired PanEnergy, one of the biggest transporters and marketers of natural gas, to form Duke Energy. Other big mergers have included Enron and Portland General, Houston Industries and NorAm Energy, and Public Service of Colorado and Southwestern Public Service Co. (to form New Century Energies). With many individual electric and natural gas companies wanting to become total energy providers, mergers or alliances will continue.

Some natural gas companies worth looking into for income (and appreciation, as they become takeover candidates) are Energen Corp. (EGN), Essex County Gas (ECGC), Piedmont Natural Gas (PNY), Questar (STR), and Washington Gas Light (WGL). All carry an S&P quality rank of A, except Piedmont, which is ranked A–.

Banks

As you can see from a quick glance at Table 2-2, Long-term Dividend Payers, banks are prominent members of that group. Their dividend history generally is positive. Lately, banks have been focusing on cost controls, loan quality, and increasing non-interest income, such as trust fees and mortgage banking income, which represents a more stable source of revenues than loans. With an oversupply of banks and fewer restrictions on interstate banking, the industry has been consolidating, which has proved to be a bonanza for shareholders of some banks that have been acquired.

In deciding which bank stocks to buy, the following measures of financial condition are useful:

- *Reserve for loan losses.* In order to cover possible future loan losses, banks are required to maintain a reserve for loan losses, which appears on the balance sheet. The reserve is a set-aside that reflects management's judgment regarding the quality of its loan portfolio, and tends to rise as asset quality deteriorates. In general, the reserve for loan losses at most banks falls within a range of 0.9% to 5% of total loans outstanding. Ratios at the top end of the range indicate that the bank has a very high level of problem loans.

- *Nonperforming loans.* The level of these loans (those in which income is no longer being accrued and for which repayment has been rescheduled) is an indication of the quality of a bank's portfolio. The ratio of nonperforming loans to total loans can range upwards from 0.5%. When it exceeds 3%, it can be a cause for concern. In addition to reducing the flow of interest income, nonperforming loans represent potential charge-offs if their quality deteriorates further.

- *Capital levels.* Banks are required by regulators to maintain minimum levels of capital. In general, the higher the capital ratio, the more conservative the bank. A higher capital ratio also indicates the ability to grow, either internally or through acquisitions.

- *Liquidity.* The extent of financial leverage, or liquidity, also says something about the relative riskiness of a bank. One measure of leverage is long-term debt divided by total equity plus total debt. For banks, a debt to equity-and-debt ratio of 50% is generally the upper limit. Banks with lower levels of debt would have room to borrow, should the need arise. A low level of debt contributes to a bank's liquidity—its ability to raise funds for lending or other purposes.

Real Estate Investment Trusts

Real estate investment trusts (REITs) afford investors an indirect means of buying a pool of professionally managed real estate assets. The assets range from health care facilities and restaurants to shopping centers and office complexes. REITs are exempt from federal corporate income taxes and most state income taxes. Requirements that must be met in order for a venture to qualify as a REIT: 95% of income must be distributed annually to shareholders in the form of dividends; at least 75% of total assets must be held in real estate or mortgages; at least 75% of revenues must be from rents on real properties or interest on mortgages secured by real property; there must be a minimum of 100 stockholders, and no five individuals may own 50% or more of the stock.

Net income is not generally used to measure the performance of a REIT mainly because for accounting purposes, the value of real estate depreciates regularly over time. Since more often than not market property values rise, the depreciation deduction from net income artificially lowers the reported earnings of REITs. The chief profitability measure is "funds from operations," similar to cash flow. Funds from operations are net income, excluding gains or losses from debt restructuring and sales of property, plus depreciation and amortization. Most REITs report both net income and funds from operations.

The average industry payout ratio (based on funds from operations) is more than 75%. A ratio above 85% to 90% could mean that the dividend may be in jeopardy. If cash flow were to suffer from an increase in property vacancies, a dividend cut could be seen.

Before you invest in a particular REIT, make sure the operators are experienced in buying and selling properties, as well as in managing them. Management should have an appreciable percentage of their net worth invested in the company. Also, avoid REITs that are highly leveraged. Cash flow should cover interest costs by a margin of at least 2 to 1.

Telephone Companies

At one time, telephone company stocks were tried and true investments for conservative income investors. The companies, notably American Telephone & Telegraph, Continental Telephone, Central Telephone & Utilities, and General Telephone & Electronics, were regulated and could be depended on for steady dividend increases and rising stock prices.

American Telephone & Telegraph was once the largest private company in the world, and "Ma Bell" paid dividends even during the Great Depression. The 1982 settlement of a Justice Department lawsuit against AT&T resulted in the breakup of the company as well as dramatic changes in the telecommunications industry.

AT&T gave up its local telephone operations in exchange for the right to compete in unregulated markets, and it agreed to transfer its holdings in the twenty-two local phone companies to seven regional holding companies (because of mergers, there are only five now) of roughly equal assets and revenues. The regionals would not be allowed to provide long-distance service, manufacture telecommunications equipment, or provide information services. (The restriction on information services was lifted in July 1991.)

The environment changed further in 1995 when AT&T decided to split into three separate companies (to provide, respectively, long distance telephone service, equipment manufacturing, and computer technology) and the telecommunications industry was on the verge of being deregulated. In late 1996, AT&T spun off to shareholders equipment manufacturing (Lucent Technologies) and computer technology (NCR).

Local telephone companies, long-distance carriers, and cable TV operators now are being allowed into each other's markets. The blurring of these different areas is reflected in the mid-1998 agreement of AT&T, the nation's largest long distance service provider, to acquire Tele-Communications, Inc., the biggest cable multiple system operator. The deal provides AT&T access to the more than 13 million homes wired by Tele-Communications.

The regional Bell operating companies, with existing lines into homes and businesses, already have a direct link to their customers. But they have never faced the fierce competition of the long-distance market. The long-distance carriers are tough competitors, and, unlike the Bells and the cable operators, have strong national brand names; however, they lack direct links to their customers. The cable operators not only have direct links, but also most of their networks are coaxial cable, which has much larger transmission capacity than the copper wire networks commonly used by the regional phone companies. Capacity is critical in providing interactive services, such as games, over these networks, but most cable transmissions are one-way: The customers can't transmit back to the cable company. The regional and long-distance telephone carriers have the essential ability to both transmit to and receive from given locations.

The bottom line is that most of the Bell regionals (Ameritech, Bell Atlantic, BellSouth, SBC Communications and US West), as well as the long distance carriers (AT&T, MCI WorldCom, and Sprint) are investing in growth opportunities, such as cellular telephones, cable, and international ventures, *and have cut back on dividend increases*. Nevertheless, the stocks as a whole remain attractive for their potential total return (appreciation plus dividends).

Summing Up

1. *Don't buy a stock on the basis of dividend yield alone.*
2. *Make sure the yield of the stock you're buying is not too far above that of other stocks in the industry.*

3. *Lean toward lower-yielding stocks with a long history of boosting dividends each year.*

4. *Look at the stock's payout ratio (dividends as a percentage of earnings). Make sure the ratio is not higher than that of the average issue in the industry group.*

5. *Check to see that the company's cash flow is at least three times its dividend payout.*

6. *For a quick check, consult the company's S&P quality ranking.*

Nobody Ever Bought Wal-Mart for Its Yield

The biggest threat you face in attempting to meet your financial goals is inflation, the continuing rise in the level of prices paid for goods and services. But why are we even talking about inflation now? Isn't that simply a relic of the early 1980s?

The consumer price index (CPI), the government's official measure of how quickly your money is losing its value, has been fairly stable in recent years. Currently, newspapers are full of stories about the lack of growth in prices. Companies are cutting staff and increasing their use of technology, always attempting to become more efficient *because they can't raise prices*. Global competition and technological innovation are driving down the cost of many goods and services, especially telecommunications services, computers, semiconductor chips, and other high-tech goods.

Overall, the CPI has risen only about 3% or less annually for the past several years, a far cry from the 13.3% jump in consumer prices the U.S. experienced during the oil crisis of 1979. Yet even at a low 3% annual increase, the average price of goods and services will still double in twenty-four years. If you're 41 now, that means prices will be twice today's level just when you're ready to retire at age 65. Today's $22,000 car would cost $44,000 in 2022, and that $7.50 movie ticket would be $15. If your child is 17 now, by the time he or she retires at age 65 in 2046, the car would cost $88,000 and the movie ticket would be $30 assuming an inflation rate of only 3% annually.

Of course, 3% inflation is fairly tame by the standards of the last two decades. Let's say inflation averages 4% for the foreseeable future. At that rate, which President Richard Nixon considered so onerous in 1971 that he imposed wage and price controls, prices double every eighteen years. At 6%, less than half the inflation rate at the peak of the last oil crisis, your purchasing power is cut in half in only twelve years. That would mean $15 movie tickets in 2010.

Experts Don't Know, Either

The point is, we don't know if the current inflation rate will persist or if it is simply a dip lasting a few years. You might be tempted to rely on the latest economic forecasts on inflation, but economists can't know the future either. If you don't believe us, save some economic predictions for a year and see how well they age. It doesn't matter if the forecasts are made by the government, private industry, or academic think tanks. Not only will economists disagree with each other, but most will be far off the mark. Consequently, forecasting inflation is little more than making an educated guess. Do you want to base your future on guesswork? You have to be ready to meet your long-term financial goals no matter what the CPI level is in coming years.

Investing in stocks with growing dividends is one of the best ways we know to beat inflation. Table 3-1 clearly shows why. In it, we demonstrate what happens to a hypothetical $10 stock that pays a $0.25 dividend when that dividend grows by 10% a year and the share price increases by the same percentage. At the end of 10 years, your current yield remains 2.5% of the most recent share price. But for long-term investors, the best way to value your dividend is to view it as a yield on your original investment. After all, though the *value* of your investment has risen over the years, *your cost has not changed.* The stock you bought for $10 is now worth $23.57, but you still paid $10 for it. And now you are getting a $0.59 annual dividend, which means that the yield on your cost is 5.9%.

A yield of 5.9% may not seem like much when you look at the recent returns of some stocks that don't pay dividends. But remember, as long as the dividend isn't cut, your annual yield on your original investment will never fall below 5.9%. In fact, if the company has a strong history of dividend increases, it is likely to go higher. And

Table 3-1. Effects of an Increasing Dividend

Year	Stock Price $	Dividend $	Current Yield %	Yield on Cost %
1	10.00	0.25	2.5	2.5
2	11.00	0.28	2.5	2.8
3	12.10	0.30	2.5	3.0
4	13.31	0.33	2.5	3.3
5	14.64	0.37	2.5	3.7
6	16.11	0.40	2.5	4.0
7	17.72	0.44	2.5	4.4
8	19.49	0.49	2.5	4.9
9	21.43	0.54	2.5	5.4
10	23.57	0.59	2.5	5.9

5.9% is more than half the average annual total return of stocks (as measured by the S&P 500 index) since 1928.

Beyond Hypothetical

Let's look at a real-world example of dividend growth. Suppose you bought 100 shares of Wal-Mart, the discount retailer, in 1973. Since the price of a stock fluctuates, let's also assume you paid the average of the high and low prices that Wal-Mart traded at during 1973. That would make your cost per share 23⅝ or $2,362.50 (excluding brokerage commission) for your "round lot" of 100 shares. At the time, Wal-Mart had been public for only a few years and was considered a fast-growing regional retailer. In 1973, the company paid its first dividend of $0.05 a share, which would have provided you with $5 on your 100 shares, or a yield of 0.2% ($5/$2,362.50) on your investment. Clearly, that yield was nothing to get excited about.

Jump ahead to the middle of 1998. Wal-Mart is the world's largest retailer, with more than 3,200 stores and warehouse clubs in the United States, Canada, Mexico, Brazil, Argentina, Germany and, through a joint venture, China. The stock's indicated annual dividend per share in 1998 was only $0.31, for a yield of 0.6% on its average share price of about 50 over the first six months of the year. Again, a yield that few would consider generous.

But we've left out a few details about Wal-Mart's rise over the 25 years since it paid its first dividend. The company increased its dividend every year and split its shares frequently. In fact, there were eight 2-for-1 stock splits in Wal-Mart shares through mid-1998. The splits turned the 100 shares you would have purchased in 1973 into 25,600 shares by 1998. Each of those shares paid a $0.31 annual dividend, resulting in a total indicated dividend payment of $7,936 for 1998. That's a dividend increase of 158,625% in 25 years. Put another way, your current dividend as a yield on your original investment is 336% ($7,936/$2,362.50). Now *that's* a yield to get excited about. And we haven't even mentioned that your initial investment of less than $2,400 had grown to be worth about $1.5 million.

By now, you're probably thinking that Wal-Mart was a great buy in 1973. But who knew? Who *could* have known? In fact, you're right. Very few people had the foresight to buy Wal-Mart stock in 1973 and stick with it for 25 years.

Yet, what if you had purchased the shares 10 years ago? At an average price of 29¼, 100 shares of Wal-Mart would have cost $2,925 in 1988. The stock paid $0.16 a share in dividends for a yield of 0.55%. By mid-1998, you would have owned 400 shares (after splits) worth about $24,000 and yielding an annual 4.2% on your original investment.

Admittedly, a 4.2% annual yield is not 336%, but it is higher than the recent inflation rate and triple the recent yield on stocks in general. What might have led you to Wal-Mart stock a decade ago? For one thing, a solid record. By then, Wal-Mart had given its shareholders 15 years of dividend increases. Although there are no guarantees, companies that regularly increase dividends are a good bet to continue doing so and are ideal for long-term investors. As legendary portfolio manager Peter Lynch notes in his book, *Beating the Street*,* "The dividend is such an important factor in the success of many stocks that you could hardly go wrong by making an entire portfolio of companies that have raised their dividends for 10 or 20 years in a row."

Table 3-2 lists 88 companies that have increased their payments to shareholders every year for the ten years through the 1998 indicated dividend. To weed out companies that make only nominal yearly dividend increases, we screened out stocks with ten-year cumulative dividend growth under 200%. That gave us a comfortable edge on inflation, which in the last decade has seen prices rise about 35%. Finally, each of the stocks in the table yields at least 3.5% on the assumed "cost" of the shares, which is their average price 10 years ago.

---

*Lynch, Peter with John Rothchild (1993), *Beating the Street*. New York: Simon & Schuster.

Table 3-2. Stocks with Good Yields on Cost

Company	Ticker	S&P Rank	1988 Average Price ($)	1998 Indicated Div. ($)	% Yield on 1988 Average Price	10-year Div. Increase (%)
Abbott Laboratories	ABT	A+	11.90	1.20	10.1	255.6
Albertson's, Inc.	ABS	A+	7.84	0.68	8.7	267.6
Alliance Capital Mgmt. L.P.	AC	NR	2.62	1.52	58.0	300.0
Analysts International	ANLY	A	1.60	0.32	20.0	253.2
Archer-Daniels-Midland	ADM	A-	5.71	0.20	3.5	517.3
Argonaut Group	AGII	B-	13.08	1.64	12.5	884.4
ASA Holdings	ASAI	A	3.02	0.44	14.6	450.0
Associated Banc-Corp	ASBC	A	7.77	0.93	12.0	229.0
Automatic Data Processing	AUD	A+	10.23	0.53	5.2	278.6
Avery Dennison Corp.	AVY	A-	11.31	0.84	7.4	211.1
BB&T Corp.	BBK	A-	11.91	1.40	11.8	258.9
Baldor Electric	BEZ	A	4.42	0.40	9.0	257.5
Banc One Corp.	ONE	A	12.08	1.52	12.6	203.0
BankAmerica Corp.	BAC	A-	6.46	1.38	21.4	360.0
Brady Corp. Cl. "A"	BRCOA	A-	7.54	0.60	8.0	480.8
Brenton Banks	BRBK	A-	2.25	0.34	15.1	274.0
Campbell Soup	CPB	B+	7.38	0.84	11.4	265.2
Charter One Financial	COFI	A-	1.90	0.56	29.5	460.0
Cintas Corp.	CTAS	A+	4.97	0.18	3.6	536.0

Table 3-2. Stocks with Good Yields on Cost *(continued)*

Company	Ticker	S&P Rank	1988 Average Price ($)	1998 Indicated Div. ($)	% Yield on 1988 Average Price	10-year Div. Increase (%)
Coca-Cola Co.	KO	A+	5.01	0.60	12.0	252.9
Cohu Inc.	COHU	A-	2.33	0.32	13.7	374.1
Compass Bancshares	CBSS	A+	6.05	1.05	17.4	214.0
ConAgra Inc.	CAG	A+	6.41	0.63	9.8	253.5
Cooper Tire & Rubber	CTB	A	5.17	0.38	7.4	340.8
CORUS Bankshares	CORS	A	6.87	0.56	8.2	460.0
Culp Inc.	CFI	A	2.92	0.14	4.8	326.8
Disney (Walt) Co.	DIS	A	15.29	0.63	4.1	447.8
Eaton Vance	EV	A-	4.81	0.48	10.0	368.3
FNB Corp.	FBAN	A-	11.15	0.72	6.5	336.4
Family Dollar Stores	FDO	A	2.04	0.18	8.8	208.7
Federal National Mortgage	FNM	A	3.40	0.96	28.2	793.0
Federal Signal	FSS	A+	4.17	0.71	17.0	294.0
Fidelity National Financial	FNF	A-	1.41	0.28	20.0	312.6
Fifth Third Bancorp	FITB	A+	5.09	0.68	13.4	300.3
First Bancorp (NC)	FBNC	NR	5.12	0.60	11.7	575.7
First Source Corp.	SRCE	A+	3.21	0.29	9.1	234.4
Firstar Corp.	FSR	A-	5.96	0.92	15.4	240.7
Fluor Corp.	FLR	A-	18.31	0.80	4.4	471.4

Company	Ticker	S&P Rank	1988 Average Price ($)	1998 Indicated Div. ($)	% Yield on 1988 Average Price	10-year Div. Increase (%)
Franklin Resources	BEN	A+	2.26	0.20	8.8	309.8
Gillette Co.	G	A+	4.89	0.51	10.4	336.5
Glacier Bancorp	GBCI	A+	2.10	0.52	24.8	271.4
Golden West Fin'l	GDW	A-	14.34	0.50	3.5	233.3
Hannaford Bros.	HRD	A	10.09	0.60	5.9	233.3
Harleysville Savings Bank	HARL	NR	3.79	0.44	11.6	254.8
Hasbro Inc.	HAS	B+	6.44	0.32	5.0	380.5
Hawkins Chemical	HWKN	A	2.04	0.20	9.8	452.5
Hewlett-Packard	HWP	A	13.65	0.64	4.7	611.1
Home Depot	HD	A+	1.22	0.12	9.8	1100.0
Huntington Bancshares	HBAN	A	6.17	0.80	13.0	202.8
Illinois Tool Works	ITW	A+	9.24	0.48	5.2	255.6
Johnson & Johnson	JNJ	A+	9.83	1.00	10.2	257.2
MBIA Inc.	MBI	A+	8.34	0.78	9.4	403.2
MYR Group	MYR	B+	1.57	0.14	8.9	937.0
MASSBANK Corp.	MASB	A-	8.99	1.00	11.1	376.2
McCormick & Co..	MCCRK	A-	5.86	0.64	10.9	276.5
Merck & Co.	MRK	A+	17.94	1.80	10.0	229.3
Mercury General	MCY	A-	3.25	0.70	21.5	559.1

Table 3-2. Stocks with Good Yields on Cost *(continued)*

Company	Ticker	S&P Rank	1988 Average Price ($)	1998 Indicated Div. ($)	% Yield on 1988 Average Price	10-year Div. Increase (%)
National Penn Bancshares	NPBC	A+	9.16	0.95	10.4	258.5
Norwest Corp.	NOB	A+	3.73	0.66	17.7	247.4
Nucor Corp.	NUE	A-	10.65	0.48	4.5	346.5
Omnicare Inc.	OCR	B+	1.81	0.08	4.4	300.0
Pall Corp.	PLL	A-	9.52	0.62	6.5	287.5
Paychex Inc.	PAYX	A	1.51	0.24	15.9	2005.3
PepsiCo Inc.	PEP	A	6.13	0.52	8.5	225.0
Pitney Bowes	PBI	A+	10.15	0.90	8.9	246.2
T. Rowe Price Associates	TROW	A	1.73	0.34	19.7	547.6
Raven Industries	RAVN	B+	5.04	0.60	11.9	252.9
Reuters Group ADS	RTRSY	NR	13.52	1.36	10.1	277.7
Reynolds & Reynolds Cl. 'A'	REY	A-	2.62	0.36	13.7	278.9
SLM Holding	SLM	A	8.94	0.56	6.3	378.2
Schering-Plough	SGP	A+	6.54	0.88	13.5	300.0
Schulman (A.)	SHLM	A	9.21	0.46	5.0	223.5
Schwab (Chas) Corp.	SCH	B+	0.76	0.16	21.1	1718.2
Shoreline Financial	SLFC	A	4.51	0.64	14.2	208.5
Star Banc Corp.	STB	A+	6.54	0.92	14.1	219.1
State Street Corp.	STT	A+	5.84	0.52	8.9	246.7

Company	Ticker	S&P Rank	1988 Average Price ($)	1998 Indicated Div. ($)	% Yield on 1988 Average Price	10-year Div. Increase (%)
Superior Industries International	SUP	A	3.35	0.32	9.6	300.0
Superior Surgical	SGC	B+	6.36	0.50	7.9	233.3
Synovus Financial	SNV	A+	2.63	0.29	11.0	364.1
Sysco Corp.	SYY	A+	4.05	0.36	8.9	679.2
Travelers Group	TRV	A+	4.12	0.50	12.1	935.2
UNUM Corp.	UNM	A-	5.75	0.59	10.3	314.0
United Asset Management	UAM	A	6.31	0.80	12.7	400.0
Valspar Corp.	VAL	A+	6.33	0.42	6.6	281.8
Wal-Mart Stores	WMT	A+	7.26	0.31	4.3	505.5
Warner-Lambert	WLA	A-	5.80	0.64	11.0	200.0
Washington Mutual	WAMU	B+	4.83	0.80	16.6	566.6
Westamerica Bancorporation	WABC	A	5.33	0.48	9.0	260.1
S&P 500			**263.15**	**16.00**	**6.1**	**56.1**

In fact, many of these stocks now provide double-digit yields on their 10-year-ago prices. Assuming there are no dividend cuts, that means owners of these stocks who have held them for a decade will outpace the average annual total return that the stock market has posted for 70 years *with just the dividends from these issues.* Again, we have not even considered the price appreciation of these stocks over the decade.

Why do these companies make regular, substantial increases in their dividends? One reason is simply that they can. Take a close look at the stocks in the table. Many are familiar names from the traditional "growth stock" universe, including Coca-Cola, Gillette, and Walt Disney Co. These are companies that consistently increase earnings. So why bother looking at dividends? Why not simply look at earnings growth to pick stocks?

Earnings growth alone can be misleading. A charge against earnings, perhaps because of an acquisition, can distort the year-to-year growth picture. What's more, owning high-growth stocks that don't pay dividends exposes your portfolio to greater volatility (as we explained in Chapter 1) and can deprive you of any returns in a bear market.

Another reason that companies pay increasing dividends is to create investor loyalty. As we have noted, a stock is less likely to be dumped by an individual who is looking forward to the next quarterly payment. And when that payment represents a double-digit return on the original investment, the incentive to hold is even greater. That helps to put a floor under the price of the stock.

When company managers own shares or receive part of their compensation in options on shares, keeping that stock price from "tanking" during a brief period of market or industry uncertainty becomes an important goal.

Does that mean that every stock in our list of 88 companies will raise its dividend annually for the next ten years? Of course not. In investing there are no guarantees. Consider Deluxe Corporation, a major check printer and supplier of computer forms and financial software. Until 1995, the company had increased its dividend for 34 consecutive years. In August of that year, the company's directors voted to keep the quarterly dividend at $0.37.

The move by Deluxe to hold its dividend steady doesn't mean that it's a bad company or that its stock is a poor investment. In fact, with some weakness in the company's businesses and an uneven earnings growth record in recent years, Deluxe directors probably made a prudent move in conserving resources by not raising the dividend. But we should note that the stock has been in a fairly narrow trading range ever since the company failed to raise its dividend. If you are looking to increase your investment returns, we suggest that you buy select companies with rising dividends. Some excellent candidates are listed in Table 3-2.

Take a close look at that list. You may be surprised to find not a single electric utility among the stocks. (Baldor Electric may sound like a power company, but it isn't. The company makes electric motors.) Although many utilities increase their dividends annually, those increases seldom outpace inflation. Utilities generally have higher *current* yields and are attractive if you need income now. But if you are planning to retire ten years or more into the future, your retirement income stream will be higher if you pick stocks that rapidly increase their dividends.

The industry group that dominates our list is financial services, with banks, insurers, and mutual fund management companies accounting for about 44% of all the stocks listed. In particular, regional banks stand out. Perhaps they increased dividends substantially because past restrictions on interstate banking prevented them from using profits to buy banks in neighboring states. As the banking industry consolidates, some of these companies will not survive as independents. But that should not stop you from investing in them, since it is likely that many will be acquired by even larger banks at a premium price.

Food and beverage companies constitute a bit more than 6.5% of our list. Among the household names in this group are Campbell Soup, Coca-Cola, ConAgra, and PepsiCo. Branded prepared food products command higher profit margins than ingredients in meals that must be made from scratch. And few industries can match the profit margins of soft drinks. When those high profit margins are made on millions of sales driven by thousands of advertising messages, significant earnings power results. Those earnings are, in part, returned to investors via steadily rising dividends.

Drug and medical supply companies make up roughly 5.5% of our list. Well-known names in this group include Abbott Laboratories, Johnson & Johnson, Merck, Schering-Plough, and Warner-Lambert. Because of patent protection on their pharmaceuticals and medical devices, these companies, too, enjoy high profit margins. Increasing dividends are the investors' reward.

The list also includes supermarket chains (Albertson's, Hannaford Bros.), other retailers (Home Depot, Wal-Mart), computer services companies (Automatic Data Processing, Paychex) and producers of plastics (Raven Industries, A. Schulman). Not all will do in the next ten years what they did in the last ten. Your best approach is to investigate the companies carefully before you invest in their stocks and to diversify across industries.

Given a choice between a high current dividend and a low, but growing one, we believe that you should always choose the latter. This simple chart (Fig. 3-1) shows you why. Let's say Tom's $100 investment returns a steady $6 annually. Jerry invests an equal amount in a stock that pays only $3 a year, but the company increases its dividend 10%

Figure 3-1

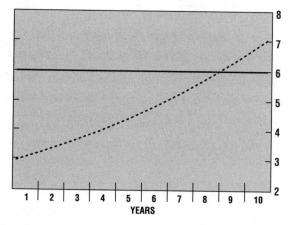

YEARS

annually. In the early years, Tom is clearly ahead. But by year nine, Jerry's annual return has outpaced Tom's and will continue to grow as compounding continues.

Summing Up

1. *You can't meet your financial goals if you don't beat inflation.*

2. *With inflation at a "low" 3% annually, prices will double every twenty-four years.*

3. *Buying stocks of companies that regularly and substantially increase their dividends is an excellent way to outpace inflation.*

4. *You should view a stock's current dividend as a yield on what you paid for the stock (your "cost basis"). Although the dividend rose, your cost didn't.*

5. *Stocks with dividends that grow into a double-digit yield on your cost outperform the historical total return of the stock market with their dividends alone.*

6. *Although most companies that have increased their dividends regularly for a decade will continue to do so, some won't.*

7. *Make sure your portfolio is diversified across several industries to avoid putting all your eggs in one basket.*

8. *Stocks that offer low current yields but increasing dividends are a better choice for long-term investors than high-yield stocks.*

"Free" 4 Stocks

The elderly widow had come to this country from Europe a half-century earlier. She and her late husband had worked hard, raised a family, and saved what they could. Over the years, she had become comfortably middle class, not rich. Certainly she would never have considered herself an "investor." Only rich people could afford to invest; she saved. Yet at some point she had bought a few shares of a gas utility and held the stock—the only one she ever owned—for the rest of her life.

In her later years, she looked forward to the dividend check that arrived like clockwork every quarter. Clearly it pleased her to have a small sum of money materialize in the mailbox four times a year. Her grandson noticed her reaction to the dividend checks and it puzzled him. A preadolescent, he was just beginning to understand how money really works. He knew the dividend checks were not his grandmother's total means of support and that the shares they represented were worth considerably more than the quarterly payments.

"Why do you keep that stock?" he asked his grandmother one day when the check arrived. "The check is only a few dollars. Wouldn't you be better off selling the shares and putting the money in the bank?"

"You don't understand, child," she answered. "Over the years, these checks have paid me back for the stock."

The story is true and the grandchild always remembered the lesson. Unfortunately, it's a lesson that few investors recognize today. And investment professionals are likely to dismiss it for two reasons, both of which make sense, and neither of which should really matter to you.

Time and Taxes

The first objection to the idea that dividends pay back your investment has to do with a concept called the "time value of money." Basically, money you have today is worth more than money you will have tomorrow. As we saw in Chapter 3, inflation eats away at the value of money, even funds that you invest. The $100 in your pocket today can be invested and earn a return, making it worth more than the $100 you get next year. The second objection is that taxes cut into the real return that dividends provide, making it take much longer for a true payback of your investment.

Essentially, both objections to the concept that dividends pay you back for the cost of your shares quibble over time. Consider a hypothetical stock that never fluctuates in price and provides a consistent 10% yield. Without taking into account the effects of inflation and taxes, this stock would pay back its cost in ten years. But an owner of the stock who is in the 28% tax bracket would receive an after-tax yield of only 7.2%. Allowing for taxes, the stock would pay back its cost in dividends in a little less than fourteen years. Similar adjustments can be made for the effects of inflation.

Maintaining Ownership

The point is not how long it takes to return your entire investment. If you are a long-term holder of a stock with a substantial or growing dividend, the point is that the cost of your investment can be returned *while you still own it.* That means you will still participate in the stock's future appreciation and dividend growth even though you have recaptured your entire original investment.

As we noted in Chapter 1, unless you want to get involved with options, the only way to realize a return on a stock that does not pay a dividend is to sell that stock. Once you sell the stock, you have created what the folks at the Internal Revenue Service call a "taxable event." Even if it's at a lower capital gains tax rate, you will have to pay taxes on your gain all at once, as we demonstrated in Chapter 1. In contrast, the dividend-paying stock spreads out your return—and the taxes on it—over time.

Table 4-1 lists a group of stocks that paid for themselves in dividends over a decade. As the "cost" of each stock, we used the average of the high and low prices in 1988. We then added up the stream of dividends for the ten years from 1989 through 1998. Since the final year of our test was not yet over when we created this list, we used the indicated dividend.

Our list eliminates stocks that sold for less than $2 (adjusted for splits) in 1988. We also left out companies that made large extra dividend payments to shareholders over the course of the decade. These were often one-time payments due to restructurings, such as the sale of a division, and don't really represent regular dividends.

Of course, you should not automatically eliminate extra-dividend payers from your portfolio. Wm. Wrigley, the world's leading maker of chewing gum, has for many years paid its shareholders a substantial *annual* extra dividend. Although Wrigley's price a decade ago was too high to be exceeded by its 10-year stream of dividends and make this list, the stock has always been one of our long-term favorites. In mid-December 1997, Wrigley paid its holders an additional $0.43 a share. That's quite a bonus considering the company's indicated dividend at the time was $0.76. Wrigley stock has paid a dividend since 1913.

With its strong dividend history, Wrigley has been a superb investment, posting a 27% average annual total return over the ten years ended 1997. Wrigley makes chew-

Table 4-1. "Free" Stocks

Company	Ticker	S&P Rank	Total Per-share Dividend Paid over 10 Years	Average Price 10 Years Ago
AEGON N.V.	AEG	NR	$ 8.91	$ 7.59
Ameren Corp.	AEE	A-	23.33	23.19
Americana Bancorp	ASBI	B+	4.29	3.94
American Health Properties	AHE	NR	22.89	17.18
Archstone Communities Trust	ASN	NR	9.89	8.88
BEC Energy	BSE	A-	17.48	15.63
BG plc ADS	BRG	NR	24.53	16.09
Bando McGlocklin Capital	BMCC	NR	8.73	6.88
BankAmerica Corp.	BAC	A-	8.15	6.46
Boddie-Noell Properties	BNP	NR	12.70	12.12
British American Tobacco ADR	BTI	NR	8.56	7.78
British Steel ADS	BST	NR	12.01	11.38
Central Hudson Gas & Electric	CNH	B+	19.97	19.37
Charter One Financial	COFI	A-	5.30	3.80
Commercial Net Lease Realty	NNN	NR	11.15	9.00
Commonwealth Energy System	CES	B+	14.94	14.88
Compass Bancshares	CBSS	A+	6.12	6.05
DQE Inc.	DQE	A	10.89	10.21
DPL Inc.	DPL	A-	7.87	7.53
DTE Energy	DTE	A-	19.58	14.75
Dynex Capital	DX	B+	9.84	4.69
Energy West	EWST	B+	3.41	3.15
Entergy Corp.	ETR	B	15.30	12.31

Table 4-1. "Free" Stocks *(continued)*

Company	Ticker	S&P Rank	Total Per-share Dividend Paid over 10 Years	Average Price 10 Years Ago
Federal National Mortgage	FNM	A	$ 5.19	$ 3.40
Federal Screw Works	FSCR	B+	10.00	8.63
Freeport-McMoRan Copper & Gold	FCXA	B+	6.27	3.04
GPU Inc.	GPU	B+	16.47	16.43
Garan Inc.	GAN	B+	11.32	10.56
General Dynamics	GD	B+	35.96	26.44
Glacier Bancorp	GBCI	A+	3.06	2.10
Great Northern Iron Ore	GNI	NR	55.50	29.93
Health Care Property Investors	HCP	NR	19.56	12.96
Health Care REIT	HCN	NR	19.32	14.56
Helix Technology	HELX	B+	3.14	2.93
Hong Kong Telecom ADR	HKT	NR	6.45	6.19
HRPT Properties Trust	HRP	NR	13.12	8.37
Indy Mac Mortgage Holdings	NDE	NR	10.20	6.44
Indiana Energy	IEI	B+	10.18	9.46
Kansas City Power & Light	KLT	B+	14.69	14.28
KeySpan Energy	KSE	B+	15.29	12.12
Marine Petroleum Trust	MARPS	NR	14.07	10.63
Meditrust Corp.	MT	NR	25.19	18.50
Mercury General	MCY	A-	3.52	3.25
Merry Land & Investment	MRY	NR	10.23	7.88
Mueller (Paul) Co.	MUEL	B-	21.00	20.63
NIPSCO Industries	NI	A	7.00	5.68
National Australia Bank ADR	NAB	NR	25.87	25.48
National Healthcare	NHC	NR	16.16	10.49

Company	Ticker	S&P Rank	Total Per-share Dividend Paid over 10 Years	Average Price 10 Years Ago
Nationwide Health Properties	NHP	NR	$12.33	$ 7.53
North Carolina Natural Gas	NCG	A-	7.52	6.94
Norwest Corp.	NOB	A+	3.86	3.73
ONEOK Inc.	OKE	B+	10.17	7.37
PG&E Corp.	PCG	B	16.34	16.19
Parkvale Financial	PVSA	A	2.63	2.54
Philip Morris Companies	MO	A+	9.81	7.60
Polaris Industries	PII	A	15.87	5.54
Rochester Gas & Electric	RGS	B	17.04	16.50
Sabine Royalty Trust	SBR	NR	14.07	12.43
Sasol Ltd. ADR	SASOY	NR	2.50	2.06
Southern Co.	SO	A-	11.75	11.12
Sturm Ruger	RGR	B+	5.80	4.78
TCF Financial	TCB	B+	2.47	2.25
UST Inc.	UST	A+	10.57	8.34
U.S. Restaurant Properties	USV	NR	11.85	9.75
United Illuminating	UIL	B	26.38	23.31
Universal Health Realty	UHT	NR	16.25	10.81
Wolf (Howard B.)	HBW	B+	2.63	2.44
Zions Bancorp	ZION	A-	2.92	2.91

ing gum in a dozen factories worldwide and sells it in 140 countries. With 50% of the U.S. chewing gum market, and a presence in the growing markets of Eastern Europe, Russia, and China, Wrigley should continue to provide investors with solid returns. But we digress. Let's take a closer look at our list of "free" stocks.

Utilities Dominate

Of the 68 companies on our list, utilities (electric and gas and companies) constitute the largest segment, at 29%. Real estate investment trusts (REITs) are next, at 22%. Why do these groups dominate this list when they don't even appear in Table 3-1, which shows stocks that have increased their dividends annually and now yield at least 3.5% on their 10-year-ago prices? The reason is quite simple. In the screen of stocks that we did for the last chapter, we were looking for companies that increased their dividends substantially over a decade. A requirement for inclusion in Table 3-1 was that a company grew its dividend by at least 200% over the course of the decade. While many utilities and REITs increase their dividends annually, they usually can't raise their payments that rapidly. On average, utilities and REITs already sport large payout ratios (dividends as a percent of earnings)—80% or more in the case of many electric utilities and 95% (by law!) for a company to qualify as a REIT. Stocks with high payout ratios can't increase dividends 200% in a decade because their earnings simply don't grow that fast.

As a result, most of the stocks in Table 4-1 are better suited to people who need current income rather than to those planning for retirement in a decade or more. In Chapter 9, we'll offer some suggested stocks for individuals who need to live on their investment income.

Financial services stocks, which include money center and regional banks, insurers, money management firms and mortgage packagers, tied with real estate investment trusts (REITs) at 22% of our list. You may recall that financial companies dominated Table 3-1 with 44% of the stocks in that group. Some of these stocks were depressed a decade ago by company-specific or industry-wide problems. But the great majority of financial services companies have enjoyed robust growth that has both boosted share prices and allowed them to raise dividends rapidly.

The last decade has seen a fairly steady decline in interest rates, which lowers the cost of capital for financial services firms. In addition, banks have shifted their operations to rely more on fee-based income rather than on earning a spread between the cost of borrowing and their lending rates. What's more, aging baby boomers are using more of the services provided by financial companies as they focus on planning their retirement. And the quest for efficiency and economies of scale has led to numerous mergers in the financial services field.

Since financial services companies dominate the list of stocks that have had strong 10-year dividend growth and tie for second place in our list of stocks that paid for themselves in dividends, you might be tempted to pick only companies from this industry for your investment portfolio. That would be a big mistake. If interest rates back up, some big mergers fail to produce the hoped-for results, or an economic downturn causes major loans to go sour, financial services companies can fall out of favor. Your best bet, as always, is to diversify your stock portfolio by industry group.

When you do put together a diversified portfolio, you should consider the following six stocks: BankAmerica, Charter One Financial, Compass Bancshares, Federal National Mortgage, Glacier Bancorp, and Mercury General. They are the only stocks to be included in both Table 3-1 and Table 4-1. We'll take a closer look at each of them.

San Francisco-based BankAmerica has agreed to merge with North Carolina-based NationsBank in a stock transaction that would form the second largest U.S. banking institution, with $570 billion in assets. The new company is set to operate under the name BankAmerica Corp. and will be a truly national franchise, serving 29 million households in 22 states. As currently constituted, BankAmerica offers deposit and lending services to individuals and small businesses through 1,800 branch offices, 970 of which are in California, its largest market. Like most large banks, BankAmerica's problem loans caused it to post losses in the mid-1980s. The company eliminated its dividend in 1986 and resumed it in 1989. Since then, BankAmerica has increased its dividend 360%, and that stream of payments exceeded the company's depressed share price a decade ago.

Charter One Financial, one of the largest thrifts in the country with assets of about $19.5 billion, recently agreed to buy Albank Financial for $870 million in stock. This latest deal makes Charter One the largest thrift institution east of the Mississippi and enhances the prospect that someday it will be taken over. Charter has grown steadily through acquisitions. Excluding merger-related charges, it has consistently increased earnings, a record that sets it apart from most companies in the thrift industry. The company was organized in 1987, paid its first dividend in 1988, and has increased its per-share payments to shareholders each year since. For the 60-month period ended June 1998, Charter One stock produced an average annual total return of more than 36%.

Compass Bancshares is a $13.8 billion bank holding company that operates 246 full-service offices in Alabama, Florida, and Texas. The Birmingham-based company also provides trust services to customers through offices in Houston and Dallas. Compass has paid dividends annually without interruption since 1939. In the five years ended 1997, the company increased its dividend by 88%. Compass has grown rapidly via acquisitions. It recently agreed to acquire Arizona Bank, which has $758 million in assets. That comes on the heels of the acquisitions of Horizon Bancorp and CFB Bancorp, both within the last two years. If you had invested $10,000 in the company's stock at the end of 1987, a decade later your position would have been worth $121,350.

Federal National Mortgage, better known in the market as "Fannie Mae," is a government-sponsored, publicly traded company that packages home mortgages as securities. In plain language, Fannie Mae buys loans from mortgage originators, bundles together those with similar characteristics, and sells these mortgage-backed securities to investors. One of the main reasons that mortgages are so easily obtainable in the U.S. is that Fannie Mae and similar organizations enable lenders to convert long-term mortgages into fresh cash that then becomes available again to home buyers in the form of new mortgages. On the other side of the equation, Fannie Mae insures the loans it packages and resells to investors against default. When investors can buy securities backed by mortgages without fear that a homeowner in a distant town may default, they are more willing to lend. That willingness is what makes the mortgage market in this country work.

Fannie Mae's success is reflected in its stock. In the five-year period ended June 1998, the stock produced an average annual total return of 31%. Earnings have risen dramatically, and dividends have grown almost 800% in the last decade.

Glacier Bancorp, a small thrift holding company in Montana, has a superb earnings and dividend history. Since it's one of the stocks we'll discuss in detail in Chapter 9, we'll just mention here that the company paid an extra dividend of $0.05 a share in January 1998. That's more than 10% of its regular annual payment to shareholders.

Mercury General provides auto insurance in California (88% of premiums), Florida, Georgia, Kansas, Oklahoma, and Texas. Although the company writes other types of policies, private passenger automobile insurance accounts for more than 90% of premiums written. Mercury tends to be selective in taking on customers. About 80% of its voluntary private passenger policies in force in California at the end of 1997 were insuring drivers in the lowest risk categories. Mercury General's dividend is up more than 559% over the last decade. For the five-year period ended June 1998, the stock provided investors with a 35% annualized total return.

Lower Yields Now

With the market surge of the past few years and a general slowdown in corporate dividend increases, it will be harder for most stocks to pay for themselves in dividends over the coming decade. Consider that typical yields on utilities fell some 40% over the last decade, from 7.1% at the end of June 1988 to 4.2% in the middle of 1998. Right now, dividend growth has slowed, in part because strong market advances keep shareholders happy. They see the prices of their stocks rising steadily and tend not to care much about dividends. Also, companies recently have been buying back their stock with funds that would normally go to increasing dividends. When a company repurchases its stock, per-share earnings and per-share book value (assets minus liabilities) rise because there are fewer shares outstanding. That, in turn, boosts the price of the stock. The price rises also because the buyback increases demand and decreases supply.

When the market once again heads south or trades in a narrow range for a long period of time, however, shareholders will demand a greater current return on their investments. That's when you can expect more frequent increases in dividends from a large number of companies.

History supports this theory. Since 1956, dividend increases on common stocks have averaged 1,699 a year. Yet in the period 1973 through 1982, which included the worst bear market in recent memory, companies averaged 2,395 dividend hikes a year—almost 41% more increases. The bull market decades immediately before and after the bear market saw average annual dividend increases of 1,563 and 1,531, respectively.

Summing Up

1. *Despite the effects of inflation and taxes, stocks with secure high dividends or steadily growing dividends will pay back their cost if held for the long term.*

2. *Traditional high-yield stocks, such as utilities and REITs, are good choices if you need current income.*

3. *Companies that have grown dividends rapidly and have paid back their cost in dividends over the last decade are particularly good choices for long-term total return. These include BankAmerica, Charter One Financial, Compass Bancshares, Federal National Mortgage (Fannie Mae), Glacier Bancorp, and Mercury General.*

4. *Slower dividend growth means that it will take longer for stocks to pay back their cost in coming years. History suggests that dividend growth should accelerate when the market advance stalls for an extended period of time.*

5
Increasing the Power of Dividends

The word "compounding" is rarely used alone in financial publications. It's preceded by either "power" or "magic," as in the power of compounding or the magic of compounding. The added nouns are not hyperbole, and we agree with the banker Baron Rothschild, who called it the eighth wonder of the world. Compounding, which is the way your investment grows as it earns returns on your initial money invested and on the interest or dividends earned, can be truly amazing. An investment of only $100 a year earning 8% will grow to $7,311 in twenty-five years, compounded annually. You will have invested only $2,500 in that time, but your earnings will total $4,811. That's an average annual return of 23.4%. If you invested $100 annually at a 10% rate, it would be worth close to $10,000 in twenty-five years, for an average return of more than 39% a year.

To figure quickly how long it would take to double your money at different rates, use the Rule of 72. Simply divide 72 by the yield. If you earn 6%, for example, it will take twelve years to double your money (72/6=12); at 7%, it will take ten years; at 8%, nine years, and so on.

To find out how long it takes to triple your money, use the Rule of 115. Divide the rate of return into 115. For example, an investment earning an 8% return will triple in 14 years. See Table 5-1 for the way the Rule of 72 works using a $1,000 investment returning 8% annually.

Reinvesting Dividends

Let's take a look at how reinvesting dividends can work its magic. The S&P 500 index, which is regarded by professional money managers as a proxy for the general mar-

Table 5-1. Compounding the "Rule of 72"

Year	Starting $ Amount	Earnings	Ending $ Amount
1	1,000	80	1,080
2	1,080	86	1,166
3	1,166	93	1,259
4	1,259	101	1,360
5	1,360	109	1,469
6	1,469	117	1,586
7	1,586	127	1,713
8	1,713	137	1,850
9	1,850	148	1,998

ket, climbed 574% over the fifteen years that ended June 30, 1998. Not too shabby. But if you plowed back the dividends, the gain nearly doubled to 985%. Put another way, if you had invested $10,000 fifteen years ago in the S&P 500 index, you'd now have $67,400. With dividends reinvested, though, that total balloons to $108,500. Over the ten years ended June 30, 1998, the S&P 500, with reinvested dividends, gained 449%, meaning that a $10,000 investment grew to $54,900. Figure 5-1 illustrates the effects of compounding on the S&P 500 stock-price index.

Although the average market returns with reinvested dividends are hefty, you would have done even better with some individual stocks. If ten years ago you had invested $10,000 in Abbott Laboratories, a maker of diversified health care products, and reinvested the dividends,

Figure 5-1

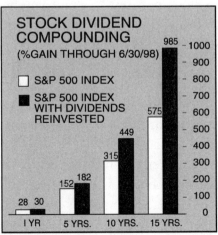

you would have $65,790 for an annual return of 23%. A $10,000 investment ten years ago in Citicorp (the parent of Citibank and the second largest U.S. bank holding company) would now be worth $98,221 with dividends plowed back. A real eye-popper is Charles Schwab, the big discount stock broker. If you had bought $10,000 worth of the stock a decade ago and reinvested the dividends, you'd now have $754,539 for an annual return of 62%. Table 5-2 lists companies in which $10,000 invested on December 31, 1987 grew in value to $75,000 or more, with dividends reinvested, on December 31, 1997.

Dividend Reinvestment Plans

More than 900 companies offer dividend reinvestment plans, or DRPs, which allow you to compound your dividends by investing them in additional shares of stock. For long-term investors, DRPs are a convenient and low-cost way to build a stock portfolio. Even if you need the dividends to live on, you can still participate in the plans. Many DRPs allow partial dividend reinvestment, whereby you can receive the dividends on a number of shares of your choosing and have the balance reinvested to buy more stock. A few plans allow you to sign up only for the optional cash payment feature, which means you can receive all the dividends.

Stocks with current high dividends or growing dividends let your capital build faster. For example, Medtronic (a producer of cardiac pacemakers and mechanical heart valves) increased its dividend 184% over the five years

Table 5-2. Stocks Posting Superior Returns with Reinvested Dividends. A $10,000 investment in any of the stocks would have grown to more than $75,00 over the last ten years. Each of these companies offers a dividend reinvestment plan (DRP).

Company	Ticker	$10,000 Became
Schwab (Charles)	SCH	$754,539
Harley-Davidson	HDI	344,526
Home Depot	HD	328,037
BankAmerica Corp.	BAC	274,702
Advanta Corp.	ADVNA	272,798
Federal Nat'l Mortgage	FNM	272,080
TCF Financial	TCB	250,092
Paychex, Inc.	PAYX	246,806
Franklin Resources	BEN	241,554
Telefonos de Mexico	TMX	230,337
Zions Bancorporation	ZION	221,274
Countrywide Credit Indus.	CCR	218,270
Intel Corp.	INTC	215,075
Albany International	AIN	211,110
Mattel, Inc.	MAT	210,091
Omnicare, Inc.	OCR	204,519
Medtronic	MDT	193,601
AEGON N.V.	AEG	191,629
Glacier Bancorp	GBCI	180,275
Frontier Insurance Group	FTR	179,770
Norwest Corp.	NOB	167,761
Merrill Lynch & Co.	MER	166,916
Gillette Co.	G	162,612
Coca-Cola Co.	KO	162,112
Cracker Barrel Old Country	CBRL	161,093
Pfizer, Inc.	PFE	159,333

Table 5-2. Stocks Posting Superior Returns with Reinvested Dividends. *(continued)*

Company	Ticker	*$10,000 Became*
Compaq Computer	CPQ	$153,117
Ciincinnati Financial	CINF	148,338
Fifth Third Bancorp	FITB	146,339
Novo-Nordisk	NVO	144,330
Newell Co.	NWL	143,739
Independent Bank Corp.	IBCP	142,874
First Commercial Corp.	FCLR	141,797
First Security Corp.	FSCO	140,341
Bank of New York	BK	137,419
UNUM Corp	UNM	136,919
First Tennessee Nat'l	FTEN	134,085
State Street Corp.	STT	133,823
Lowe's Companies	LOW	132,277
Schering-Plough Corp.	SGP	131,119
Allied Group, Inc.	GRP	129,787
MacDermid, Inc.	MRD	130,923
First Commerce	FCOM	129,453
Washington Mutual	WAMU	129,189
M&T Bank	MTB	128,930
Crompton & Knowles	CNK	127,143
Star Banc Corp.	STB	125,099
Synovus Financial Corp.	SNV	123,872
Pioneer Hi-Bred Int'l	PHB	122,590
Clayton Homes	CMH	121,467
Compass Bancshares	CBSS	121,350
Blount, Inc	BLT.A	119,112
Computer Associates	CA	115,458
Southtrust Corp.	SOTR	113,947
Firstar Corp.	FSR	113,618
Reynolds & Reynolds	REY	110,671
Wells Fargo	WFC	110,171

Company	Ticker	$10,000 Became
First Fin'l Holdings	FFCH	$109,596
Kansas City Southern Industries	KSU	108,361
Lancaster Colony Corp.	LANC	107,030
Mercantile Bancorp	MTL	104,875
Westamerica Bancorp	WABC	103,550
AMCOL Int'l	ACOL	103,340
PaineWebber Group, Inc.	PWJ	102,690
Deposit Guaranty Corp.	DEP	102,687
Commerce Bancorp (N.J.)	CBH	102,488
Popular, Inc.	BPOP	101,321
SunTrust Banks, Inc.	STI	101,037
Comerica, Inc.	CMA	100,952
Campbell Soup Co.	CPB	100,928
Mellon Bank Corp.	MEL	99,837
ReliaStar Financial	RLR	99,161
Servicemaster L.P.	SVM	98,629
Donaldson Co	DCI	98,590
Citicorp	CCI	98,221
Nationsbank	NB	97,819
Old Kent Financial	OKEN	97,469
Smith (A.O.) Corp.	AOS	96,940
St. Paul Bancorp	SPBC	96,560
Huntington Bancshares	HBAN	96,377
Colonial BancGroup	CNB	95,898
Chase Manhattan	CMB	95,786
Regions Financial Corp.	RGBK	95,531
INMC Mortgage Holdings	NDE	94,241
Colgate-Palmolive	CL	94,023
Warner-Lambert	WLA	93,964
Walgreen Co.	WAG	93,915
Kennametal Inc.	KMT	93,227
Lilly (Eli)	LLY	92,046
Procter & Gamble	PG	91,712

Table 5-2. Stocks Posting Superior Returns with Reinvested Dividends. *(continued)*

Company	Ticker	*$10,000 Became*
Century Telephone	CTL	$91,419
Philip Morris Cos.	MO	90,024
Dayton Hudson Corp.	DH	89,968
Fiirstbank of Illinois	FBIC	89,945
Jefferson-Pilot Corp.	JP	89,769
NIPSCO Industries	NI	89,589
Household International	HI	89,560
Citizens Banking	CBCF	89,307
Old Republic International	ORI	87,830
Diebold, Inc.	DBD	87,774
National Commerce Bancorp	NCBC	87,672
Union Planters Corp.	UPC	87,462
Albertson's Inc.	ABS	85,528
Kuhlman Corp.	KUH	85,279
Marshall & Isley Corp.	MRIS	85,159
General Electric	GE	85,157
Wrigley (Wm.) Jr.	WWY	85,024
Tyco International	TYC	84,782
Johnson & Johnson	JNJ	83,920
RLI Corp.	RLI	83,397
Interpublic Group	IPG	82,952
Pioneer Standard Electric	PIOS	81,800
Illinois Tool Works	ITW	81,786
U.S. Bancorp	USB	81,469
Mylan Laboratories	MYL	81,468
Amsouth Bancorp	ASO	81,372
Provident Companies	PVT	80,767
Aon Corp.	AOC	80,114
Associated Banc-Corp.	ASBC	79,018
BB&T Corp.	BBK	77,647
AFLAC Inc.	AFL	77,494

from 1993 through 1997, with $10,000 invested at the end of 1987 worth $193,601 on December 31, 1997, a 39% annual rate of return. Motorola's dividend, which is up 118% in the five years through 1997, helped the stock attain a 20% annual rate of return over the 1987–1997 period.

Many brokers will now reinvest dividends for you on any stock without a fee. They do not, however, permit you to take advantage of a DRP's optional cash purchase feature. This valuable feature permits you to send in money (usually, the minimum amount is low and the maximum is fairly high) on a periodic basis to purchase shares at little or no transaction cost.

Another valuable aspect of some DRPs is the reinvestment of dividends at a discount from the market price. About 70 companies offer a discount, ranging from 1% to 10%. Most are banks, utilities, and real estate investment trusts (REITs), which need a large amount of capital to conduct their businesses. DRPs are an inexpensive way for these companies to raise capital (new shares are issued for the plans rather than purchased from the open market). For a list of companies offering discounts, see Table 5-3.

Of course, you can also receive the benefits of compounding via mutual funds. Funds—both open-end (which continuously issue shares to accommodate new investors or existing investors who are adding money to their accounts) and closed-end (which have a relatively fixed number of shares that trade on the open market as any other stocks)—offer shareholders

Table 5-3. DRP Stocks Offering Discounts

Company/Ticker	Discount (%)
American Realty Trust/ARB	10
American Water Works/AWK	2
Aquarion Co./WTR	5,5*
Atmos Energy/ATO	3
Ball Corp./BLL	5
Bayview Capital/BVCC	5
Berkshire Gas/BGAS	3, 3*
Blount, Inc./BLT.A	5, 2*
Bradley REIT/BTR	3,3*
Carolina First/CAFC	5
CBL & Associates/CBL	5
CNB Bancshares/BKN	3
Colonial Gas/CLG	5
Commerce Bancorp/CBH	3, 3*
Continental Mortgage & Equity Trust/CMETS	5
Countrywide Credit/CCR	2
Cousins Properties/CUZ	5
Crestar Financial/CF	5
Duke Realty /DRE	4
Essex County Gas/ECGC	5
E'Town Corp./ETW	5,5*
F&M Bancorp/FMBN	5
First American Corp./FATN	5
First Commercial Corp./FCLR	5
First of America/FOA	5
First Union Corp./FTU	1
Fleming Cos. /FLM	5
Fuller (H.B.) /FULL	3
Green Mountain Power/GMP	5

Company/Ticker	Discount %
Health Care REIT/GCN	4,4*
Hibernia Corp./HIB	5
Household International/HI	2.5
IMPAC Mortgage Holdings/IMH	3
Independent Bank Corp./IBCP	5
IPL Energy/IPPIF	5
Kennametal/KMT	5
Lafarge Corp./LAF	5
Liberty Property/LRY	3
Media General/MEG.A	5
Mercantile Bankshares/MRBK	5
Merry Land & Investment/MRY	5, 5*
Monmouth Real Estate/MNRTA	5, 5*
National City Corp./NCC	3, 3*
New Plan Realty/NPR	5
North Carolina Natural Gas/NCG	5
Old National Bancorp/OLDB	3
ONEOK/OKE	3
Piccadilly Cafeterias/PIC	5
Piedmont Natural Gas/PNY	5
Popular/BPOP	5
Presidential Realty /PDL.B	5
Public Service Of North Carolina/PGS	5
ReliaStar Financial/RLR	4
Second Bancorp/SECD	5
Shoreline Financial/SLFC	5
Southwest Water/SWWC	5
Suffolk Bancorp/SUBK	3, 3*
Telephone & Data Systems/TDS	5
Time Warner/TWX	5
Transcanada Pipelines/TRA	5
Union Planters/UPC	5

Table 5-3. DRP Stocks Offering Discounts *(continued)*

Company/Ticker	Discount %
United Mobile Homes/UMH	5
Unocal Corp./UCL	1
UtiliCorp United/UCU	5
Valley Resources/VR	5
Westcoast Energy/WE	5
York Financial/YRK	10

*Discount on optional cash payments.

the option of reinvesting dividends, as well as any capital gains distributions.

Many DRPs and most mutual funds permit you to invest via automatic withdrawals from checking or savings accounts each month. That not only helps in the compounding process but also encourages disciplined investing, which is the key to a successful financial future.

Investing a set amount each month, moreover, allows you to purchase fractional shares as well as full shares. In other words, you invest in dollars rather than shares. Dollar-cost-averaging comes into play here, which we will discuss in Chapter 7.

An increasing number of companies permit you to bypass the broker entirely when you buy their shares. Sign up for the DRP, and you can buy your first shares directly from the company. Table 5-4 lists companies that will let you buy initial shares from them, along with the minimum investment to open a DRP account.

Table 5-4. Where Initial DRP Shares May Be Purchased Directly

	Minimum Purchase
Advanta Corp./ADVNA	$1,500
AFLAC Inc./AFL	750
AGL Resources/ATG	250
Air Products & Chemicals/APD	250
Ameritech/AIT	1,000
Amoco/AN	450
Amway Asia Pacific/AAP	250
Arrow Financial/AROW	300
Atmos Energy/ATO	200
Bank of New York/BK	1,000
Bard (C.R.)/BCR	250
Barnett Banks/BBI	1,000
Becton, Dickinson/BDX	250
Bell Atlantic/BEL	1,000
BellSouth/BLS	500
Bob Evans Farms/BOBE	50
Boston Beer/SAM	500
BRE Properties/BRE	500
Carpenter Technology/CRS	500
Central & Southwest/CSR	250
Central Hudson Gas & Elec./CNH	100
Chevron/CHV	250
Chock Full O'Nuts/CHF	250
CILCORP/CER	250
CMS Energy/CMS	500
Coastal Corp./CGP	250
Comsat/CQ	250
Cross Timbers Oil/XTO	500
Crown American Realty Trust/CWN	100
Curtiss-Wright/CW	2,000

Table 5-4. Where Initial DRP Shares May Be Purchased
Directly *(continued)*

	Minimum Purchase
Dayton Hudson/DH	$ 500
Deere & Co./DE	500
Dominion Resources/D	250
DQE Inc./DQE	105
DTE Energy/DTE	100
Duke Realty Investments/DRE	250
Eastern Co./EML	250
Energen/EGN	250
Enron Corp./ENE	250
Entergy/ETR	1,000
Equifax/EFX	500
Equitable Cos./EQ	500
Exxon/XON	250
Federal Nat'l Mortgage/FNM	250
Finova Group/FNV	500
First Commercial/FCLR	500
First Financial Holdings/FFCH	250
Food Lion/FDLNA	250
Ford Motor/F	1,000
Frontier Insurance/FTR	100
Gencorp/GY	500
General Electric/GE	250
Gillette/G	1,000
Goodyear Tire & Rubber/GT	250
Guidant/GDT	250
Harland (John H.)/JH	500
Hawaiian Electric/HE	100
Hillenbrand Industries/HB	250
Home Depot/HD	250

	Minimum Purchase
Houston Industries/HOU	$ 250
International Business Machines/IBM	500
Illinova/ILN	250
Interchange Fin'l Svcs./ISB	100
Investors Fin'l Svcs./IFIN	250
Ipalco Enterpirses/IPL	250
Johnson Controls/JCI	50
Justin Industries/JSTN	500
Kaman Corp./KAMNA	250
Kellwood/KWD	100
Kerr-McGee/KMG	750
Libbey/LBY	100
Liberty Property Trust/LRY	1,000
Lilly (Eli)/LLY	1,000
Longs Drug Stores/LDG	500
Lucent Technologies/LU	1,000
Madison Gas & Electric/MDSN	50
Mattel/MAT	500
McDonald's/MCD	1,000
MCN Energy/MCN	250
Meadowbrook Insurance/MIG	250
Mellon Bank/MEL	500
Mercantile Bancor./MTL	500
Merck & Co./MRK	350
MidAmerican Energy/MEC	250
Midsouth Bancorp/MSL	1,000
Minnesota Power & Light/MPL	250
Mobil/MOB	250
Montana Power/MTP	100
Morgan Stanley Dean Witter/MWD	1,000
Morton Int'l/MII	1,000

Table 5-4. Where Initial DRP Shares May Be Purchased
Directly *(continued)*

	Minimum Purchase
Nationsbank/NB	$1,000
Nationwide Financial Svcs./NFS	500
New England Business Svc./NEB	250
Newport News Shipbldg./NNS	500
Northwestern Corp./NOR	500
Norwest/NOB	250
OGE Energy/OGE	250
Old Nat'l Bancorp/OLDB	500
ONEOK/OKE	100
Owens Corning/OWC	1,000
Pacificorp/PPW	500
Penney (J.C.)/JCP	250
Peoples Energy/PGL	250
Pharmacia & Upjohn/PNU	250
Philadelphia Suburban/PSC	500
Phillips Petroleum/P	500
Piedmont Natural Gas/PNY	250
Pinnacle West Capital/PNW	50
Procter & Gamble/PG	250
Providian Financial/PVN	500
Public Service Entpr./PEG	250
Public Service of New Mex./PNM	50
Public Service of NC/PGS	250
Quaker Oats/OAT	500
Questar/STR	250
Reader's Digest/RDA	1,000
Regions Financial/RGBK	1,000
Roadway Express/ROAD	250
Rockwell Int'l/ROK	1,000
SBC Communications/SBC	500

	Minimum Purchase
Scana Corp./SCG	$ 250
Sears, Roebuck/S	500
Sierra Pacific Res./SRP	50
Snap-on/SNA	500
Southern Co./SO	250
Synovus Financial/SNV	250
Tandy Corp./TAN	250
Taubman Centers/TCO	250
Tektronix/TEK	500
Tenneco/TEN	500
Texaco/TX	250
Timken/TKR	1,000
TNP Enterprises/TNP	100
Transocean Offshore/RIG	500
Tribune Company/TRB	500
Tyson Foods/TSN	250
U S West/USW	300
United Wisconsin Svcs./UWZ	100
Utilcorp United/UCU	250
Valspar Corp./VAL	1,000
Walgreen/WAG	50
Wal-Mart/WMT	250
Warner-Lambert/WLA	250
Weingarten Realty/WRI	500
Western Resources/WR	250
Whitman Corp./WH	250
WICOR Inc./WIC	500
Wisconsin Energy/WEC	50
WPL Holdings/WPH	250
WPS Resources/WPS	100
York International/YFED	1,000

IRAs and Compounding

The magic of compounding works especially well with an Individual Retirement Account (IRA). A person who contributes $2,000 annually (the maximum allowed, unless one is married and files a joint return, in which case the maximum is $4,000) will accumulate $297,200 after thirty years, assuming a 9% annual return (stocks historically have returned an average of almost 11% annually). In a taxable account, assuming a 28% tax rate, the amount would be only $183,300.

If you fund a traditional IRA partially or entirely with appreciating stocks that don't pay dividends, the tax-deferred compounding advantage may be significantly offset by the loss of capital gains tax treatment when it comes time to take distributions. Your IRA withdrawals are taxed as ordinary income, unless you have a Roth IRA (see below). You can start distributing at age 59½ if you wish, but the first distribution from a traditional IRA must be made by April 1 of the year after you reach age 70½ and the second by December 31 of that year. Distributions from Roth IRAs can be made after age 70½. The minimum traditional IRA distribution can be based on the combined life expectancies of the IRA owner and a younger designated beneficiary, and during such a span, Congress could easily increase the tax bite on ordinary income and/or diminish the capital gains tax break.

Another disadvantage of funding an IRA with stocks: You can't deduct investment losses realized in the account. Without that restriction, IRAs would be ideal for investors who trade stocks frequently, incurring losses as well as short-term gains that would otherwise be taxed at ordinary income rates. However, by holding IRA stocks for long periods, ten years or more, you substantially reduce the risk of incurring nondeductible losses in the account.

The Roth IRA, which became effective in 1998, is more attractive than the traditional IRA since distributions after age 59½ are tax-free if the Roth is held more than five years. Distributions before age 59½ are tax-free if the IRA is held more than five years and the owner dies, becomes disabled or uses proceeds (up to a $10,000 lifetime maximum) for a first-time home purchase. As with a traditional IRA, you can contribute up to $2,000 to a Roth, or $4,000 for married couples (less any amounts contributed to traditional IRAs). You are not eligible for a Roth, however, if you're single and your adjusted gross income is more than $110,000 or, if you're married and filing jointly, more than $160,000.

Dividend-Paying Stocks in IRAs

High-yield stocks, and particularly stocks with steadily increasing dividends, are good IRA funding choices for most investors. For accounts that will remain largely undistributed for fifteen or twenty years or longer, portfolios consisting entirely of dividend-paying stocks with growth potential can be expected to outperform portfolios balanced with stocks and fixed-income investments. The tax deferral not only accelerates dividend yield compounding, it also postpones taxes when you sell long-time holdings with huge gains—and then spreads any tax bite over your distribution years.

A convenient way to set up a self-directed IRA is via dividend reinvestment plans. Brokerage houses normally won't offer to act as a custodian for an IRA with a DRP since they don't get commissions when stocks are purchased in a plan. At this writing, 22 companies currently permit IRAs in their DRP plans, and the list is growing.

Companies now offering the IRA option are: American Electric Power (1-800-328-6955), Ameritech (1-800-233-1342), Atmos Energy (1-800-382-8667), Bell Atlantic (1-800-631-2355), Chrysler (1-800 649-9896), Connecticut Energy (1-800-736-3001), Connecticut Water (1-800-426-5523), Exxon (1-800-252-1800), Federal National Mortgage (1-888-289-3266), Ford Motor (1-800-279-1237), GTE Corp. (1-800-225-5160), Houston Industries (1-800-231-6406), Lucent Technologies (1-888-582-3686), McDonald's (1-800-621-7825), Mobil (1-800-648-9291), Morton International (1-800-446-2617), OGE Energy (1-888-216-8114), Philadelphia Suburban (1-800-205-8314), SBC Communications (1-888-836-5062), Sears, Roebuck (1-800-732-7780), UtiliCorp United (1-800-884-5426) and Wal-Mart (1-800-438-6278).

The question often arises whether it pays to contribute to an IRA if you cannot deduct the contributions on your income tax return. Unless you're not covered by a qualified pension plan or are a relatively low-income taxpayer (for 1998, adjusted gross income [AGI] of no more than $60,000 on joint returns or $40,000 on single returns), you'll get no deduction for IRA contributions. The Roth IRA is not deductible under any circumstances. But even if you can't deduct your funding, it still pays to set up a traditional nondeductible IRA. Invested in dividend-paying growth stocks or mutual funds, $2,000 can, compounded tax-free, create a sizable nest egg. And although there is some paperwork involved (you must file IRS Form 8606, "Nondeductible IRA Contributions, IRA Basis, and Nontaxable IRA Distributions" with your income tax return), it is far from burdensome.

Summing Up

1. *Compounding truly is magic. Your investment grows as it earns returns on the initial money invested and on the interest or dividends added.*

2. *To find out quickly how long it would take to double your money at different rates, use the "Rule of 72." Just divide 72 by the yield.*

3. *If you reinvest your dividends via dividend reinvestment plans, your stake in a particular company can grow dramatically over time. If you need some income, most DRPs allow you to put only some of your shares into the plans.*

4. *Traditional individual retirement accounts (IRAs) receive an extra lift from compounding because they grow tax-free until withdrawal. With a Roth IRA, there are no taxes at*

withdrawal if you're at least 59½ and have held your account for at least five years.

5. *Dividend-paying stocks are excellent choices for IRAs.*

6. *Even if you can't deduct your IRA contributions on your income tax return, they are still worthwhile.*

Dividend **6** Investing via Mutual Funds

It's safe to say that, were it not for mutual funds, millions of people of modest means would not have enjoyed the benefits of equity investing. As we pointed out earlier, stocks have outperformed other types of investments over the long term by a good margin. Enthusiasm for funds has spilled over to more affluent investors, who regard mutual funds, rightly so, as a good way to diversify their portfolios.

Reflecting their popularity, the mutual fund industry has mushroomed from sixty-eight funds in 1940 (when Congress passed the Investment Company Act) to almost 7,000 in mid-1998 (3,203 stock funds, 2,228 bond funds, 518 hybrid funds and 1,027 money market funds). Assets have rocketed from $448 million in 1940 to more than

$3.5 trillion. According to the Investment Company Institute, the trade group for the fund industry, more than 66 million individuals in 32% of U.S. households, own mutual funds. Some expect that by the year 2000, individuals will have more money in mutual funds than in bank savings accounts and CDs.

Besides their relatively low purchase minimums and the fact that subsequent small sums may be added on a regular basis, mutual funds offer the smaller investor diversification, which reduces risk. An added plus is professional management for those who don't have the time or inclination to look after their own portfolios. Although the pros don't often outperform the market, many do a creditable job.

Funds for the Dividend-Oriented

Income investors can choose various mutual funds that invest in money market instruments, bonds, and/or preferred stocks (fixed-income funds) or in a combination of stocks and bonds (balanced funds). These funds' main objective is income, with capital gains a secondary consideration. For those looking for a combination of income and capital appreciation, two fund categories fit the bill: growth and income funds (also called "large blend") and equity income funds (also called "large value," as well as "income").

Growth and Income

This type of fund aims for steady, if not high, income payouts, while placing equal weight on capital appreciation. Many of the stocks in the S&P 500 index can be found in growth and income funds. The majority of the funds are large-cap portfolios with various percentages in different industries (known as sector weightings). Growth and income funds are less susceptible to short-term economic-cycle and sector shifts. Growth and income funds generally seek growth of capital and current income. They primarily invest in equity securities with above-average yields and potential for appreciation. The price-earnings ratios of the stocks in growth and income funds typically are below that of the S&P 500 index. Morningstar, which ranks mutual funds, calls these funds "large blend."

Equity Income

Equity income funds, which are also known as large value or income funds, seek relatively high current income and growth of income by investing 60% or more of their portfolios in equities. Risk is generally low. Managers of equity income funds generally attempt to provide yields that are at least 50% higher than the yield of the S&P 500. Big dividend payers, such as the major oil companies, drugs, and utilities, can be found in the typical equity income portfolio. An equity income fund seeks income by typically investing in equity securities with above-average yields.

Despite the conservative nature of growth and income funds and equity income funds, studies have shown that, over the longer term, they come close to matching the performance of more aggressive funds, such as growth and small-cap. The dividend-oriented funds, moreover, have achieved their strong records with fewer down years and less steep declines than the more aggressively oriented funds.

Before we talk about specific growth and income and equity income funds, a word on load vs. no-load funds is in order. We believe unequivocally that no-load funds are your best bet. Your broker, of course, will not agree.

By buying a fund with no sales charge, you are not only saving on the commission, but all of your money goes into the fund as well. For example, $10,000 invested in an 8.5% front-end load fund results in an $850 sales charge and only a $9,150 investment in the fund. The load actually represents 9.3% of the net funds invested. If a load fund is held for many years, the effect of the load, if paid up front, is not diminished as quickly as many believe. If the money paid for the load had been working for you, as in a no-load fund, it would have been compounding over the entire period.

Some experts say load vs. no-load isn't an important issue, and that the key to picking a fund is performance. We maintain that for every strong-performing load fund, there is a similar no-load or low-load fund.

Keep in mind that funds have various ways of tacking on sales charges. At one time, an 8.5% front-end sales commission was common. Currently, the number of funds charging the full 8.5% load is diminishing. Some funds sold by brokerage firms have lowered their front-end commissions to 4% or less, and others have introduced back-end loads, deferred sales charges, or redemption fees, all of which mean you pay when you sell the fund. The 12b-1 fee, named for the section of the Investment Company Act that permits it, has also become popular. It allows the fund's investment advisor to use fund assets to pay for distribution costs, including advertising, distribution of fund literature, and sales commissions paid to brokers.

Some funds use 12b-1 fees as load charges in disguise. Since the charge is annual and based on the value of the investments, a high 12b-1 fee can result in total costs to long-term investors that are higher than the old 8.5% up-front sales load, yet allowing the fund to be classified as no-load. Make sure you check the fund prospectus for any charges that are imposed. More and more funds have been offering a choice of sales charges, but the classifications are far from standardized. Class A shares generally have front-end loads, Class B shares typically have a 12b-1 charge and a declining back-end load, and a Class C may be offered with a level load.

Fund expense ratios include 12b-1 fees and other charges for portfolio management and administrative, legal and other costs, but not sales charges. Equity fund expense ratios range from 2.75% or more for some international funds with high expenses to 0.20% or less for some of the passively managed index funds.

The current trend among mutual funds is to build assets, since management fees are based on a percentage of a fund's total assets. Thus, an increasing number of funds have tried to gather more assets by reducing front-end charges.

Favored Growth and Income Funds

The following growth and income type funds have good long-term performance records and impose no sales charges or other fees, except for reasonable management fees.

- **AARP Growth & Income Fund** emphasizes high-yield stocks to meet its goal of capital growth and current income. It picks stocks on the basis of relative dividend yields rather than on price-to-earnings or price-to-book ratios. The fund only buys stocks whose yields are at least 20% higher than that of the S&P 500 index. An issue is sold when its dividend yield drops below 75% of the S&P 500's yield. The fund is often invested in out-of-favor stocks and industries and has shown low volatility over the years.
  Five-year average annual return (through May 31, 1998): 20.9%
  Management fee: 0.48%
  Minimum initial investment: $500
  Telephone: 1-800-322-2282

- **Babson Value Fund** follows a value-oriented investment strategy. The fund looks for undervalued stocks, using price-to-book and price-earnings measures. The portfolio usually is made up of stocks that are out of favor with investors. The fund does not usually invest in companies rated below B– in investment quality by S&P. The average price-earnings multiple in the portfolio typically is among the lowest in the growth and income fund category.

Five-year average annual return (through May 31, 1998): 22.2%
Management fee: 0.95%
Minimum initial investment: $1,000
Telephone: 1-800-422-2766

- **Columbia Common Stock Fund** looks for growth of capital and dividends. It invests at least 65% of its assets in common stocks of large, well-established companies. For the five years ended May 31, 1998, Columbia Common Stock Fund had an average annualized total return of 19.1%, compared with a total return of 18.8% for all Large-Cap Value funds. The fund ranked 102 within the entire universe of 231 funds in the peer group, according to Morningstar.
Five-year average annual return (through May 31, 1998): 19.1%
Management fee: 0.60%
Minimum initial investment: $1,000
Telephone: 1-800-547-1707

- **Dodge & Cox Stock Fund** invests in companies that are currently out of favor. The fund looks for companies that have the potential for positive earnings surprises. A "bottom-up," or company-specific, approach is used. Stocks in the portfolio have below-average price-earnings ratios, price-to-book ratios, and market-capitalization-to-sales ratios. Investments are made with at least a five-year time horizon, and the turnover rate is low (below 20%). Because the fund sells only a few holdings per quarter, it is tax efficient.

Five-year average annual return (through May 31, 1998): 20.3%
Management fee: 0.50%.
Minimum initial investment: $2,500
Telephone: 1-800-621-3979

- **Fidelity Growth & Income Fund** seeks long-term capital growth, current income, and growth of income consistent with reasonable risk. It invests primarily in securities of companies that pay current dividends and offer potential earnings growth. Generally, the fund sells stocks with dividends that fall below the yield of the S&P 500 index. It employs a bottom-up strategy, buying stocks that are inexpensive relative to their historical price-earnings ratios and price-to-cash flow ratios. Over the past ten years, the fund ranked number five within the 52 funds in its peer group, according to Morningstar.
  Five-year average annual return (through May 31, 1998): 21.2%
  Management fee: 0.72%
  Minimum initial investment: $2,500
  Telephone: 1-800-544-8888

- **Janus Investment Fund** seeks long-term growth consistent with preservation of capital. The fund invests basically in common stocks of larger, well-established companies, although it may invest in stocks of any size. It may also invest in preferred stocks, warrants, government securities, and corporate debt. James P. Craig has managed the fund since 1986.
  Five-year average annual return (through May 31, 1998): 18.2%

Management fee: 1%
Minimum initial investment: $2,500
Telephone: 1-800-525-8983

- **Lexington Corporate Leaders Fund** seeks long-term capital growth and income. The fund is unusual in that, at its inception in 1935 the advisor, Lexington Management Corp., selected a group of thirty blue chip companies to comprise a permanent portfolio, holding an equal number of shares of each company. If a stock splits, those shares are sold and redistributed among the other positions in the portfolio. The fund is barred from adding new positions. The only exception is in the case of a spinoff. Since its inception, the fund has eliminated several companies from the portfolio because of restructurings or because they stopped meeting criteria for industry leadership. For the ten-year period ended May 31, 1998, the fund ranked 29 within the 123-fund universe of the peer group, according to Morningstar. The fund will cease operations on November 30, 2001.
  Five-year average annual return (through May 31, 1998): 19.4%
  Management fee: 0.40%
  Minimum initial investment: $1,000
  Telephone: 1-800-526-0056

- **Scudder Growth & Income Fund** seeks capital growth and current income through high-yielding stocks. The fund believes that a stock's yield is a better valuation tool than its price-earnings ratio. As a result, many of the issues are out of investor favor. Stocks are purchased only when yields are at least 20% higher than that of the S&P 500 index. A stock will be sold when its yield falls to 75%

of that of the S&P 500 index. The fund's emphasis on yield has resulted in solid returns and below-average risk. Five-year average annual return (through May 31, 1998): 20.7%

Management fee: 0.60%

Minimum initial investment: $2,500

Telephone: 1-800-225-2470

- **T. Rowe Price Dividend Growth Fund** seeks to provide increasing dividend income and long-term capital appreciation. The fund invests primarily in established, well-managed companies whose earnings and dividends have grown steadily over the years and are expected to continue to do so. In operation only since 1992, the fund has recorded an above-average return.

  Five-year average annual return (through May 31, 1998): 21.1%

  Management fee: 0.48%

  Minimum investment: $2,500

  Telephone: 1-800-638-5660

- **T. Rowe Price Growth & Income** seeks long-term growth of capital, current income, and an increase in future income. The fund invests most of its assets in stocks of companies with earnings that are sufficient to support a growing dividend. Up to 30% of assets may be invested in convertible and corporate debt securities and preferred stocks. A strict value approach is used, with high-growth issues generally avoided. Overweighting in a particular sector is also avoided.

  Five-year average annual return (through May 31, 1998): 17.9%

Management fee: 0.60%
Minimum initial investment: $2,500
Telephone: 1-800-225-2470

- **Vanguard Growth & Income** (formerly Vanguard Quantitative) seeks a total return greater than that of the S&P 500 index. The fund has a diversified portfolio similar to the S&P 500 in terms of dividend yield, price-earnings ratio, return on equity, and price-to-book ratio. At least 65% of assets are invested in securities that are included in the S&P 500. The fund emphasizes conservatism. It seeks to achieve consistent positive returns while avoiding large losses during market downturns. For the ten years ended May 31, 1998, the fund ranked nine within its 92-fund peer group, according to Morningstar.
Five-year average annual return (through May 31, 1998): 22.2%
Management fee: 0.30%
Minimum initial investment: $3,000
Telephone: 1-800-662-7447

Favored Equity Income Funds

The following equity income funds, which are also called large value or income, boast above-average performance records and carry no sales charges or other fees, except for management fees.

- **Fidelity Equity Income II** invests at least 65% of its assets in dividend-paying stocks. A value-oriented fund, Fidelity Equity Income II looks for issues that have relatively low price-earnings and price-to-book ratios. Financial stocks normally make up a large chunk of the portfolio. Foreign stocks may also be heavily weighted in the portfolio.

Five-year average annual return (through May 31, 1998): 19%

Management fee: 0.52%

Minimum initial investment: $2,500

Telephone: 1-800-544-8888

- **Harbor Value's** objective is maximum long-term total return. The fund typically invests at least 65% of assets in dividend-paying stocks, although it may invest up to 15% in non-dividend-paying stocks. Harbor emphasizes issues that it believes are undervalued. For the ten-year period through May 31, 1998, the fund ranked 46 out of its 123-fund peer group, according to Morningstar.

  Five-year average annual return (through May 31, 1998): 19.8%

  Management fee: 0.60%

  Minimum initial investment: $2,000

  Telephone: 1-800-422-1050

- **Oakmark Fund** looks for long-term capital appreciation and income. The fund invests primarily in common stocks and convertibles. Oakmark concentrates on issues that offer good long-term value. According to Morningstar, the fund ranked near the top of its peer group for the five years ended May 31, 1998.

  Five-year average annual return (through May 31, 1998): 22.4%

  Management fee: 1%

  Minimum initial investment: $1,000

Telephone: 1-800-625-6275

- **T. Rowe Price Equity Income** seeks dividend income and capital appreciation. It invests at least 65% of assets in dividend-paying stocks of well-established companies. The balance of assets are invested in preferred stocks or investment-grade fixed-income securities. Large-capitalization stocks that are undervalued or out of favor figure prominently. Risk is below average.

  Five-year average annual return (through May 31, 1998): 19.7%

  Management fee: 0.50%

  Minimum initial investment: $2,500

  Telephone: 1-800-638-5660

- **Vanguard Equity Income Fund** aims to provide its investors with yields above that of the S&P 500. The fund concentrates on well-established, large-capitalization stocks that are out of investor favor, though the companies' fundamentals and finances are strong enough to support their dividends.

  Five-year average annual return (through May 31, 1998): 18.9%

  Management fee: 0.78%

  Minimum initial investment: $3,000

  Telephone: 1-800-662-7447

Closed-End Funds

Unlike open-end mutual funds that issue and redeem shares at net asset value, or NAV (the total market value of all stocks held divided by the number of fund shares outstanding), closed-end funds don't redeem shares. They increase shares outstanding only when raising new capital through secondary offerings, and they can buy back shares on the open market. Since supply and demand determine their share prices, closed-end funds may sell at discounts or premiums to NAV. The funds are traded like individual stocks on the exchanges and over-the-counter.

With closed-end funds, managements are not forced to sell low as investors exit a falling market or buy high with new money. These funds can take a longer-term view than mutual funds that are subject to net redemptions, and they can also hold illiquid stocks that might put other funds in a bind.

Three closed-end funds that have large-cap dividend-oriented stock portfolios and that sell at discounts are **Adams Express, Tri-Continental Corp.,** and **Nations Balanced Target Fund.** Nations Balanced aims to return principal by maintaining half the portfolio in zero-coupon Treasury notes; the other half is in blue chip stocks. The fund matures on September 30, 2004, when management expects to return at least the $10 per share provided by original investors who reinvest all dividends and hold to maturity.

The financial pages of newspapers generally list closed-end fund NAVs only weekly, but the major closed-end funds calculate NAV daily, and provide it as part of a toll-free phone service. A separate listing of closed-end funds can be found in *Standard & Poor's Stock Guide.* The listing offers uniform data on more than 500 closed-end funds in twenty-four investment categories.

Summing Up

1. *Mutual funds are a good way for smaller dividend-oriented investors to invest. Funds also are attractive for larger investors because they offer diversification.*

2. *Growth and income funds (also called "large blend") and equity income funds (also called "large value" or "income") are the two major categories of funds for those mainly interested in dividend income.*

3. *Although growth and income funds and equity income funds are conservative and carry relatively small risk, they have done just as well as the more aggressive, riskier funds over the long term.*

4. *We recommend you buy only no-load (no sales charge) funds. By purchasing funds that don't have sales charges, not only do you save on the commission, but all of your money goes into the fund as well. We also recommend you avoid funds that have 12b-1 fees and other charges.*

5. *Favored growth and income funds are AARP Growth & Income, Babson Value, Columbia Common Stock, Dodge & Cox Stock, Fidelity Growth & Income, Janus Investment Fund, Lexington Corporate Leaders, Scudder Growth & Income, T. Rowe Price Dividend Growth, T. Rowe Price Growth & Income, and Vanguard Growth & Income. Favored equity income funds are Fidelity Equity Income II, Harbor Value, Oakmark Fund, T. Rowe Price Equity Income, and Vanguard Equity Income.*

6. *Consider conservative, blue chip, closed-end funds that sell at a discount. Examples are: Adams Express, Tri-Continental, and Nations Balanced Target.*

7
Dividend Strategies

In Chapter 5, we took a look at how reinvesting dividends can fatten your portfolio over time. We spoke about how dividend reinvestment is convenient and low-cost. Another benefit of reinvesting your dividends is that it allows you to take advantage of dollar-cost-averaging. This is one of several strategies we'll examine in this chapter.

Dollar-Cost-Averaging

Every investor is looking for an easy way to do well in the market. Dollar-cost-averaging is perhaps the best known "easy" or mechanical way to invest. The strategy offers you the potential for profits with reduced market risk. It frees you of the problems of attempting to time market fluctuations (which studies show is a futile effort), and, in fact, puts those swings to work for you.

Dollar-cost-averaging simply entails buying a fixed dollar amount of a stock at specific time intervals. You buy fewer shares when the price is high and more shares when it is low. Over the years, your average cost per share using this formula method of investing will be lower than the average of your purchase prices, providing the stock is in a basic long-term uptrend.

See Table 7-1 for an example of how dollar-cost-averaging works. If you invest $600 a month for three months and the purchase price of the stock for each of the three months is $25, $20, and $30 a share, respectively, your total investment of $1,800 buys 74 shares at an average cost of $24.32 a share (before commissions). If you had invested the $1,800 in a lump sum at the average price of $25, you would have bought only 72 shares. The advantage would have been the same had the price pattern been $30, $25, $20; $20, $25, $30; or $20, $30, $25.

Dollar-cost-averaging enables you to turn the market's movements to your advantage over a period of time.

Table 7-1. Dollar-Cost-Averaging

Months	Investment	Share Price	Number of Shares
1	$600	$25	24
2	600	20	30
3	600	30	20
		$25 Avg. Price	
	Total: $1,800		74 shares
Average cost per share: $1,800/74 = $24.32			

Overall, you should achieve solid long-term investment results. Remember, though, the key to success is "stick-to-itiveness." Don't be scared off when the market is in a downtrend. Regard a period of falling stock prices as an opportunity to buy a larger number of shares of an issue that will likely climb in the not-too-distant future.

Stocks that pay dividends and have a history of regularly increasing payments are especially good for dollar-cost-averaging. This type of stock can help to provide a regular money flow for periodic investments, particularly when you have an unexpectedly large bill due that makes it difficult to come up with the money you need to invest. To get the most out of your dollar-cost-averaging plan, you should start to invest before a stock sells ex-dividend (the buyer of a stock selling ex-dividend, meaning without the dividend, does not receive the recently declared dividend; rather, the payment goes to the seller). Check *Standard & Poor's Stock Guide* for ex-dividend dates.

Dow Dividend Strategy

Another formula investing method that has proven itself over the years is the Dow dividend strategy, or the Dogs of the Dow, as it is popularly known. The strategy is simplicity itself. At the end of every year, buy the ten highest-yielding stocks of the thirty in the Dow Jones Industrial Average, putting equal amounts of money into the ten issues. Hold the stocks until the end of the following year, and repeat the process.

The strategy historically has done better than the Dow Jones Industrial Average as a whole. Over the past 60 years, the Dow dividend strategy has not only outperformed the Dow index and the S&P 500, but also just about every other investment strategy. According to O'Shaughnessy Capital Management, a money management company based in Greenwich, Connecticut, $10,000 invested on December 31, 1928 in the ten-highest yielding stocks in the Dow annually rebalanced (replacing stocks that no longer qualified with those that did) would have been worth $41,325,595 on December 31, 1997. By comparison, $10,000 invested in the S&P 500 index in that period would have been worth $8,296,378. The strategy works well even in bad markets. In the worst market period since World War II (1973–1974), the ten top-yielding Dow stocks were up slightly vs. a 40% plunge in the S&P 500.

You can find a list of the stocks in the Dow Industrials in *The Wall Street Journal*. The newspaper runs the names in the daily market chart in Section C. At this writing, the thirty issues in the index are the following:

AT&T	Coca-Cola
AlliedSignal	Disney (Walt)
Aluminum Co. of America	DuPont
American Express	Eastman Kodak
Boeing	Exxon
Caterpillar	General Electric
Chevron	General Motors

Goodyear	Morgan (J.P.)
Hewlett-Packard	Philip Morris
IBM	Procter & Gamble
International Paper	Sears, Roebuck
Johnson & Johnson	Travelers Group
McDonald's	Union Carbide
Merck & Co.	United Technologies
Minnesota Mining & Mfg.	Wal-Mart

At the end of 1997, the top ten Dow yielders were (in order of highest yields): Philip Morris, J.P. Morgan, General Motors, Chevron, Eastman Kodak, Exxon, Minnesota Mining & Manufacturing, International Paper, AT&T, and DuPont.

What's the Secret?

Why does the Dow dividend strategy work so well? Perhaps it's because the prices of the highest-yielding stocks in the Dow are depressed. More often than not, however, the issues offer good value. They are all well-known, large-capitalization stocks of companies that, for the most part, are not likely to go out of business. Usually, company-specific problems that have caused investors to shun the stocks can be fixed. Or it may be just a question of time before unfavorable industry conditions can be reversed, such as high interest rates that would adversely affect financial stocks or a recession that would depress cyclical stocks.

In the meantime, you are receiving above-average dividend yields. (Even though Woolworth [now Venator Group and no longer in the index], one of the Dow top yielders for 1994, omitted its dividend in April 1995, investors in the Dow dividend strategy still received a solid average yield from the other nine stocks.) Keep in mind that dividends have historically accounted for more than 40% of the average total return on all of the Dow stocks.

Variations on a Theme

Some variations on the Dow dividend strategy have sprung up. One is the "Flying Five," in which you buy the five lowest-priced stocks among the ten Dow high yielders. This approach has actually done better than the top ten approach, according to O'Shaughnessy Capital Management. The "Flying Five," however, carries more risk, since you don't have as much diversification as with the top ten Dow yielders.

There is also the strategy that calls for buying only the five top-yielding stocks in the Dow. The return on the top five since 1928—14.6%—about matches that of the top-yielding ten stocks. Here again, you are less diversified.

In following the Dow dividend strategy, you don't necessarily have to start on December 31. You may use any day of the year as your anniversary date. To rebalance every twelve months, sell those stocks that no longer are among the Dow's ten highest yielders. Of the stocks that carry over into the new year, buy or sell a few shares until each of the stocks has the same dollar value and put the same amount into each of the new stocks. Of course, you're not going to get an exact allocation, but a small variance does not affect results significantly.

The Dow Dividend Strategy via UITs

The Dow dividend strategy has proven so popular that a number of brokerage houses now offer unit investment trusts based on the strategy. (Unit investment trusts, in contrast to continually managed mutual funds, are unmanaged fixed portfolios of stocks or bonds that are held for a specified term.) Offered by a consortium of four major brokers: Merrill Lynch, Salomon Smith Barney, Morgan Stanley Dean Witter, and PaineWebber, the UITs are called the Select Ten portfolio. The UITs are invested in the ten highest-yielding Dow stocks and then turned over twelve months later. Small investors might consider the Select Ten UITs, since they can be purchased for as little as $1,000, or $250 for IRAs. Although there are fees (typically a 1% sales charge and 1.75% in annual management fees), they are lower than what it would cost you to buy small amounts of stocks in ten companies from a broker.

Dow Dogs Mutual Funds

Over the past two years, some Dow dogs mutual funds have sprung up. They are not pure plays, however, since the SEC does not allow mutual funds to limit investments to ten companies. The most prominent of these funds are: Hennessy Balanced (1-800-966-4354), which invests half of its assets in the ten Dow dogs and the rest in one-year Treasuries; O'Shaughnessy Dogs of the Market (1-800-797-0773), which places half of its assets in the Dow's ten highest yielders and the rest in 20 high-yielding stocks from the S&P Industrials; and Payden & Rygel Growth & Income (1-800-572-9336), which invests half of its assets in the Dow dogs and the other half in the S&P 500 index. All three funds are no-loads (no sales fees are charged).

Geraldine Weiss' Theory

Editor and publisher of the newsletter *Investment Quality Trends* (twice-monthly, $275 a year, phone 619-459-3818), Geraldine Weiss has for 30 years been championing the theory that a stock's underlying value is in its dividends, not in its earnings. She emphasizes that blue chip companies are more predictable than are newcomers or companies with erratic records of earnings and dividends. A blue chip is defined as stock of a company that (1) has raised its dividend at least five times in the past twelve years, (2) has at least five million shares outstanding, (3) has at least eighty institutions holding its stock, (4) has seen earnings improve in at least seven of the last twelve years, (5) has a record of at least twenty-five years of uninterrupted dividends, and (6) has a Standard & Poor's ranking of A or A+.

According to Ms. Weiss' theory, a stock's price is driven by its yield. When a stock offers a high dividend yield, investors will buy, which results in a higher price and a lower dividend yield. When the yield declines, the stock will languish until it falls far enough to make the yield attractive again.

Ms. Weiss' research has shown that stocks typically fluctuate between extremes of high dividend yield and low dividend yield. These recurring extremes can be used to establish a channel of undervalued and overvalued prices. The tops and bottoms of cycles are determined by charting the dividend yield of a stock over a long enough period of time for the dividend-yield pattern to emerge. By calculating the historic points at which a stock turns down, or reverses a slide and turns up, the future behavior of that stock can be anticipated. Ms. Weiss runs charts of many stocks in her books, *The Dividend Connection* (Dearborn Financial Publishing, Inc., 1995) and *Dividends Don't Lie* (Longman Financial Services Publishing, 1988).

Relative Dividend Yield

The relative dividend yield strategy, as espoused by Anthony Spare, a money manager based in San Francisco, is similar to Geraldine Weiss' technique. The two most common measures of whether a stock is overvalued or undervalued are the price-earnings ratio (the current price of the stock divided by its earnings per share for the last twelve months or estimated earnings for the next twelve months) and book value (assets minus liabilities). Instead, Spare's strategy calls for comparing the stock's dividend yield with the yield of the Standard & Poor's 500 index. If a stock's yield is considerably higher than that of the index, the stock is a buy.

To calculate the relative dividend yield, divide the yield of the S&P 500 into the stock's yield. When the result is well above 1 (the yield is more than 100% of that of the S&P 500), it is a signal to buy the stock. As in the Dow dividend strategy and Ms. Weiss' approach, most of the stocks with buy signals are depressed and the companies are encountering difficulties, usually temporary. But the investor is compensated for being patient by a good dividend stream, as is the case with the other dividend strategies.

Summing Up

1. *Dollar-cost-averaging (buying a fixed-dollar amount of a stock at specific intervals) is a disciplined way to invest and makes market fluctuations work for you. Stocks that pay dividends and have a history of regularly increasing payments are especially good for this strategy, since they can help to provide a regular money flow for your periodic investing.*

2. *The Dow dividend strategy, in which you buy the ten highest-yielding stocks in the Dow Jones Industrial Average at the end of each year, has handily beaten the market over the past sixty years.*

3. *For small investors, Dow dividend strategy unit investment trusts (called the Select Ten) are a smart buy.*

4. *Variations on the Dow dividend strategy include buying the five lowest-priced stocks among the ten Dow high yielders or buying the top five Dow yielding stocks. Mutual funds that invest half of their assets in the ten highest-yielding Dow stocks are another variation on a theme. These approaches have recorded impressive results.*

5. *Aids to determining when to buy or sell stocks are Geraldine Weiss' technique of dividend yield patterns or Anthony Spare's relative dividend yield (comparing a stock's yield with that of the Standard & Poor's 500 index).*

8

Profits from Dividend Cuts

Back in Chapter 2 we warned you never to buy a stock on the basis of its dividend yield alone. Nothing we will say in this chapter contradicts that basic rule. Remember that it's still important to look before you leap into an investment. Strange as it may seem, most people do more research before buying a refrigerator for a few hundred dollars than they do before buying a stock for several thousand dollars. But as we saw in the last chapter, higher yields can lead you to higher total returns simply by pointing you toward stocks that have become undervalued.

A Fear of Cuts

One reason that yields of some utility stocks are very high is that investors, believing that the dividends are in danger of being cut, simply avoid these issues. That may not always be a wise move. A twenty-year simulation for the period that ended February 28, 1992 pitted the five highest-yielding issues in the S&P utilities index against the broad market as represented by the S&P 500. The five highest-yielding utilities were "purchased" and held for a year. A stock was "sold" at the end of the holding period if it was no longer one of the top five in yield. Allowing for commissions of 1%, this trading approach to high-yielding utility stocks produced an annualized return of 13.2% vs. 11.4% for a "buy and hold" strategy using the S&P 500. Returns for both strategies are with dividends reinvested.

If this sounds a bit like the methodology behind the Dow dividend strategy that we described in the last chapter, that's because it is. Both techniques rely on the market's tendency to overreact. In general, investors either "love" or "hate" a particular stock at any given time.

The utilities study was conducted by our colleague David Braverman, senior investment officer at Standard & Poor's, and was published in S&P's weekly investment advisory newsletter, *The Outlook* on May 6, 1992. Braverman notes several general reasons that the total return of utilities was greater than that of the broad market over the twenty-year test. During periods of high inflation, many utilities are able to pass along a large portion of their increased operating costs to their customers. Yet, during recessions (there were four during the twenty-year period), commercial and industrial demand for power drops less than demand for cyclical goods such as steel. Consequently, earnings of utility companies are less volatile than those of many other industries.

Utility stocks also tend to behave differently at market extremes. In bull markets, they lag as investors chase stocks of companies that post strong earnings growth or bid up takeover candidates. In bear markets, however, the higher yields of utilities tend to provide support for the shares while other stocks tumble.

But why did the *highest-yielding* utilities beat the general market in the twenty-year simulation? When the market believes that a company is about to cut its dividend, it drives the price of the stock down. That, in turn, raises the current yield. There are really only two possibilities: The dividend is cut or it isn't. If it's cut soon after you purchase the stock, you'll probably suffer a paper loss as the value of the shares declines. On the other hand, if the dividend is trimmed after a long stretch of time, you will have had the benefit of an above-average yield for an extended period. The other possibility is that the dividend is never cut. In this case, you will have collected an above-average yield and probably will have seen a large capital gain once the market realizes that the risk of a dividend cut has passed.

Buying on the Cut

In his study, Braverman noted that a case could be made that a utility stock's rebound is faster if the dividend is reduced, since the lower payment to shareholders can help to improve the company's balance sheet and its financial flexibility. We decided to take a closer look at that idea by tracking the performance of electric companies that actually had cut their dividends.

As you might remember, in Chapter 1 we told you about FPL Group, a Florida-based electric utility holding company that cut its annual dividend from $2.48 to $1.68 in 1994, even though it had increased the payment annually for the preceding 48 years. We noted that the stock plunged almost 14% on the day of the announcement. What we didn't say was, had you bought FPL after that price decline and held it for a year, your investment would have appreciated 37%. And even with the reduced dividend, the total return for the year was well over 40%. Could this indicate a pattern among electric companies that cut their dividends?

To find out, we looked at major power companies that cut or omitted their dividends between 1985 and 1994. Right away, we discovered that omission of a dividend did not bode well for the utility's share price. Shares of four of the seven power companies that eliminated their dividend payments during that decade were lower a year later and posted an average loss of 57%. One stock was essentially unchanged and only two were higher in price. Our conclusion: You don't want to risk buying shares of an electric company in such bad shape that it must completely eliminate its dividend.

Table 8-1 shows the twenty-five dividend cuts by twenty-three electric utilities (Centerior Energy, which has since merged with Ohio Edison to form FirstEnergy, and Energy East each cut twice in the decade), arranged by date. If you had purchased the shares at the closing price on the day of the cut (or, if the cut was announced after the market close, at the closing price on the next trading day) and held it for a year, on only seven occasions (28% of the time) would you have lost money. The average loss was 24.2%. But on another four tries (16% of the time), the share price would have been essentially flat after a year. For this study, we defined flat as within $0.50 of the starting price.

That left fourteen gains in our study. Although the average share price appreciation was 23.3%, the chances of producing a gain (14 out of 25, or 56%) were little better than a coin toss.

Improving the Odds

Unless you thrive on casino-style risk, odds that are only slightly better than 50-50 are not worth your hard-earned money. But take a closer look at Table 8-1 and a pattern may start to emerge. Note that as the decade turned, more electric utility dividend cuts became profitable for people who bought after the announcement.

There were a dozen cuts from 1985 through 1989. Five of the stocks were lower a year later and another

Table 8-1. Electric Utilities That Cut Dividends 1985-1994

Dividend Cut Date	Stock	% Gain or Loss One Year Later
1994		
Oct. 14	Energy East	35.7
Aug. 16	TNP Enterprises	13.4
June 17	Edison International	24.5
May 9	FPL Group	37.0
Jan. 4	Centerior Energy*	−29.4
1993		
Dec. 15	Central Maine Power	−16.0
Feb. 17	PacifiCorp	flat
1992		
Sept. 10	Unicom	27.0
July 10	Sierra Pacific Resources	18.4
1991		
June 18	Eastern Utilities Assoc.	19.0
1990		
Aug. 21	Ohio Edison*	15.4
April 23	PECO Energy	28.6
Feb. 7	Portland General**	6.0
1989		
Dec. 24	BEC Energy	flat
Aug. 22	Tucson Electric Pwr.	−53.7
1988		
Dec. 22	Pinnacle West Capital	−29.4
June 28	PG&E Corp.	29.4
April 26	Pub. Ser. New Mexico	−27.3
March 22	Centerior Energy	flat
Jan. 15	Energy East	12.0

Dividend Cut Date	Stock	% Gain or Loss One Year Later
1987		
Dec. 18	Central Hudson G&E	14.0
Sept. 16	Rochester G&E	flat
July 23	Niagara Mohawk Pwr.	−6.7
1986		
April 18	DQE	−11.6
1985		
May 6	Kansas City P&L	45.9

*Merged in November 1997 to form FirstEnergy Corp.
**Acquired by Enron Corp. in July 1997.

three were flat. In other words, you did not make a profit in eight of twelve instances, or almost 67% of the time. Fast forward to the 1990s. Of the thirteen electric power companies that cut their dividends from 1990 through 1994, ten were higher in price a year later. That means people who bought on the dividend cut made a profit almost 77% of the time. Buying on the bad news worked much better in the 1990s than it did in the 1980s. Buy *why?*

One possible explanation is that the interest rate environment of the 1990s helped. Utility stocks are often considered "bond surrogates" and, like fixed-income securities, rise in value as interest rates decline. For most of the first three years of this decade, interest rates fell, causing bonds and utility stocks to rise. Could this be the reason that even though the electric utilities in question cut their dividends, their share prices advanced?

Table 8-2. Performance of Dividend-cutting Electric Companies vs. S&P Utilities Index. Between 1990 and 1994, the ten electric utilities that cut their dividends and rose in price outpaced the utilities market in the year following the reduction.

Dividend Cut Date	Stock	% Gain One Year Later	% Gain in S&P Utilities Index	% Advantage of Stock over Index
1994				
Oct. 14	Energy East	35.7	19.7	81.0
Aug. 16	TNP Enterprises	13.4	7.6	76.0
June 17	Edison International	24.5	7.9	210.0
May 9	FPL Group	37.0	10.3	259.0
1992				
Sept. 10	Unicom	27.0	20.5	31.7
July 10	Sierra Pacific Resources	18.4	15.2	21.0
1991				
June 18	Eastern Utilities Assoc.	19.0	8.1	134.0
1990				
Aug. 21	Ohio Edison*	15.4	7.6	102.0
April 23	PECO Energy	28.6	3.6	694.0
Feb. 7	Portland General**	6.0	flat	...

*Now part of FirstEnergy
**Acquired by Enron

Table 8-2 shows the ten electric utilities that rose in price after cutting their dividends between 1990 and 1994 and the change in value of the S&P utilities index over the same one-year periods. Nine of the ten stocks advanced when utility stock prices were rising. In one case, the index was virtually flat after a year. But in each of the ten cases, the share price performance of the company that had cut its dividend was better than the advance in the utilities index over the same period. While utilities in general went nowhere (as measured by the index), the shares of Portland General rose 6% for the year ended February 7, 1991. The outperformance was even more dramatic when the utilities index rose in price. In the nine instances of rising utility share prices, the stocks of the power companies that cut their dividends rose from 21% to 694% more than the index. The average outperformance was 178.7%.

A Tale of Two Decades

If these stocks didn't simply move with the utilities group on interest rate declines, why did they do better in the 1990s than in the 1980s? We believe that the market is viewing many electric utility dividend cuts in the current decade as aggressive and preemptive, while dividend reductions in the 1980s were seen as defensive and a reaction to events not under the power companies' control.

Much of the history of electric power in the 1980s was influenced by an event that occurred before the decade began. The accident at Three Mile Island in

Pennsylvania in 1979 changed Americans' perception of nuclear power forever. Not a single new nuclear plant has been ordered in the U.S. since that accident. But before that incident, the U.S. electric power industry was enthusiastically building nuclear plants. Following the oil shocks of 1973 and 1979, electric utilities preferred to rely on nuclear energy rather than on imported oil to generate power. Consequently, a large number of nuclear plants were under construction when the Three Mile Island accident occurred. Some would be mothballed at great cost to the power companies that had begun to build them.

Many of the electric companies that cut their dividends in the 1980s did so because uncompleted nuclear plants had sapped their financial strength. Regulators were often unwilling to have the ratepayers bail out power companies that had made huge bets on nuclear plants. Instead, the shareholders paid by having their dividends cut.

The 1990s brought a new problem to the electric power industry: the threat of competition. Ever since Thomas Edison first wired lower Manhattan in the late 19th century, electric power has been considered a "natural monopoly." Generally, that meant it would be prohibitively expensive to set up two or more companies selling the same service in a particular territory. So, in place of competition, government regulators set the prices that customers would pay. But in recent years, other natural monopolies have fallen in the face of evidence that competition brings lower prices and better service. Long-distance and local phone service are now open to competition. Why not electric power?

A major step in the direction of open competition in the electric utility industry was the October 1992 passage of the National Energy Policy Act (NEPA). NEPA allowed federal regulators to authorize utilities to provide transmission service for any power generator (either another utility or an independent power company) to another electric utility. Although NEPA specifically prohibited authorizing transmission that would bypass the local utility to sell power to an end-user, most observers of the industry thought it would just be a matter of time before that was allowed, too.

Seven electric utilities cut their dividends between the passage of NEPA and the end of 1994. Four of the stocks were higher a year later, two were lower and one was essentially unchanged. On the surface, it looks as if we're back to a coin toss, since investors using a buy-on-the-cut strategy made money only 57% of the time.

But note some of the comments made by officials of these power companies when they cut their dividends. Three companies (Centerior Energy, TNP Enterprises, and Energy East) cited the likelihood of "increased competition." Although it did not specifically mention potential competition, FPL Group sounded a similar note, saying that a high dividend payout "takes away our financial flexibility." Edison International (then known as SCEcorp) cut its dividend by 30% two months after California regulators submitted a proposal that would allow every electricity consumer in the state to pick a power supplier by the year 2002. The company cited "uncertainty about the outlook" for future utility income.

In contrast, Central Maine Power and Sierra Pacific Resources made no mention of potential competition or the need to be more flexible. Central Maine cut its dividend 43% because regulators approved only part of the rate increase it sought. Sierra Pacific cut its dividend 39% because it needed to improve its capital position in light of a lower allowed rate of return. Shares of both Central Maine and Sierra Pacific were lower a year after they cut their dividends.

Of the five companies that appeared to be getting their financial houses in order to prepare for the future, only Centerior Energy saw its shares lower a year after the dividend cut. In less than four years, Centerior no longer existed as a separate company. The other four (80% of the total) had higher share prices a year after they reduced their dividends. The average appreciation was 27.7%.

Since our study of the effects of dividend cuts on electric company share prices ended in 1994, we wanted to update it for the paperback edition of this book. Consequently, we looked at major power companies that cut their dividends in 1995 and 1996 to see how their share prices fared a year later.

The first major power company to cut its dividend over the two-year period was Texas Utilities. On October 16, 1995, the company cut its quarterly payment to stockholders by 35% to $0.50 a share. At the time of the cut, the company indicated that it was conserving cash to fund attractive investment opportunities. At least some investors knew what the company meant; the stock actually rose almost 4% on the day of the cut. It rose another 8.7% over the next year, outpacing the 5% gain in the S&P utilities index. For more on the attractive investment opportunities Texas Utilities found, see Chapter 9.

The next power company we considered was Northeast Utilities, which serves some 1.7 million customers in New England from its base in Hartford. On July 23, 1996, the company slashed its dividend 43% to $0.25 a share. The stock fell 4.6% that day, not much of a drop for so large a dividend cut. The reason was that investors, expecting the dividend to be trimmed, had already pushed the shares down 52% from their 1996 high of 25¼. Regulators, citing safety concerns, had shut down all three of the company's Millstone nuclear power plants by the end of March. In July, the Connecticut Yankee plant also was shut down. Northeast Utilities cut its dividend to conserve cash. A year later, the stock was at 9¾, representing a decline of 15.7% from the closing price on the day the dividend was cut. One reason that the stock tumbled over the course of that year was that Northeast's problems persisted, and the company eliminated its dividend in early 1997.

The third major utility to cut a dividend during the period was PG&E Corporation, then known as Pacific Gas & Electric. The company took action less than a month after California Governor Pete Wilson signed legislation that began the process of deregulating the state's power industry. On October 19, 1997, PG&E reduced its quarterly payment from $0.49 to $0.30 a share. Since the cut came on a Friday after the market close, we looked at the stock's price action on the following Monday. Investors appeared to have anticipated the reduction; the stock was unchanged for the day. In the press release announcing the dividend reduction, PG&E did say it wanted to "repurchase common stock, retire debt, and fully pursue new growth opportunities." But that statement followed a rather long discussion of how earnings would be lower with deregulation and "under greater pressure from the competitive marketplace." A year later, although the stock had risen 4.4%, the S&P utilities index had gained 8.8%

True to form, shares of the power company that reduced its dividend to invest in new opportunities had the best performance and outpaced the S&P utilities index. The company that cut because of problems saw its shares lower a year later. The most difficult to evaluate was PG&E, which cut because of the pressures of impending deregulation, but also indicated that it wanted to explore other opportunities. Although investors did bid up the shares over the following year, they did so with little enthusiasm.

We should caution you that, while our study of electric utilities that cut their dividends to improve competitiveness strongly suggests that their stocks usually rise, our sample was very small. Since this is a rather new phenomenon, further studies will be needed to confirm our findings. We believe (and the evidence so far seems to confirm) that when electric utilities tell you they are reducing dividends to improve future results, it sends a strong signal that the market usually likes. Nevertheless, buying a stock on the news of a dividend cut remains an aggressive trading strategy. If you decide to attempt it, realize that you are taking a greater risk than you would in investing in a stock that steadily increases its dividend.

Summing Up

1. *Some utility stocks sport high yields because investors, fearing dividend cuts, avoid them.*

2. *Picking the highest-yielding utilities annually and holding them for a full year provided a greater total return than the market in a twenty-year simulation.*

3. *If a utility's dividend isn't cut, shareholders benefit from the higher yield. If it is, the share price often rebounds quickly.*

4. *In recent years, shares of electric utilities that cut dividends to prepare for increasing competition usually were higher in price a year later.*

9

Selected Stocks Worth Buying

$\mathbf{B}$y now, we hope you are convinced that our strategy of buying quality stocks that have good dividend records is a solid way to invest for the long term. So far in this book, we've given you lists of hundreds of stocks that fit various dividend criteria. Some readers will consider these lists as raw materials for a creative search to find the stocks that best suit their needs. Others may just find the sheer number of interesting stocks overwhelming.

If you're in the second group, the twenty-three thumbnail sketches of stocks that follow may help you narrow the field. We've divided them into four separate groups. Some equities clearly fit into more than one category. We made the final selection in each group with an eye toward industry diversification.

Although we find these stocks attractive for the long haul, don't simply take our word for it. Check out recent developments in each company either through a recognized research service (see Appendix A for some sources) or by reading the company's latest SEC filings. We've included addresses and phone numbers for each company so that you can follow up on your own.

We've included historical data on dividend growth and total return through the end of 1997. For comparison, the benchmark S&P 500 index posted an annualized total return of 18.1% for the ten years ended December 31, 1997. We deliberately left out valuation measures such as P/E ratio (price-earnings, or how much you are paying for each dollar of expected company earnings) and current yield. Since these measures depend on a stock's price on any given day, we've left it up to you to decide if the stocks are attractive for purchase when you read this book. We've included a chart of each stock's monthly price action for the three years ended early July 1998.

Group I: Stocks You Can Buy Directly

The following suggested stocks are for younger investors who are employed and don't depend on dividend income to meet living expenses. Each of the companies profiled permits you to bypass a broker and to buy shares directly, if you join its dividend reinvestment plan. Each also permits regular optional cash payments. As we saw in Chapter 5, DRPs are a convenient and inexpensive way to build a portfolio.

The six stocks make up a diverse group, with representation in entertainment, oil, restaurants, consumer products, banking, and technology. We believe they have above-average long-term earnings and dividend growth prospects.

Disney (Walt)

500 S. Buena Vista St.
Burbank, CA 91521
1-800-948-2222 (Plan Agent)

DIS/New York Stock Exchange
Dividends paid since 1957
S&P earnings and dividend ranking: A
Indicated annual dividend as of June 30, 1998: $0.21
Increase in dividends from 1993 through indicated 1998: 173%
$10,000 invested on 12/31/87 worth on 12/31/97 with
dividends reinvested: $70,599
Ten-year annualized total return: 24%

Disney's diverse operations include filmed entertainment, broadcasting, theme parks and retail stores. The addition of an animal theme park in Florida in mid-1998 should boost the number of visitors and their average length of stay at the Walt Disney World complex. Disney also owns about 30% of Euro Disney, a French company that operates the Disneyland Paris theme park business. Disney is planning a $1.4 billion expansion of the Disneyland theme park resort in Anaheim, California. The expansion, expected to be completed in 2001, will include a new theme park called Disney's California Adventure, and a 750-room hotel.

In 1996, the company acquired broadcaster and publisher Capital Cities/ABC for cash and stock valued at about $20 billion. Disney divested much of Capital Cities' print operations in 1997. The broadcast segment includes the ABC television network, various TV and radio stations and 80% ownership of cable network ESPN.

With its strong franchise in family entertainment, Disney is well situated for the multimedia age ahead. Growing income levels in foreign markets should increase future demand for Disney-related products. Per-share earnings increased at an average annual rate of 16% over the past five years through 1997. Investors, however, should view the company's per-share profits on an adjusted basis; that is, adding back the large amount of noncash amortization related to acquisitions. For 1998, estimated amortization is $0.62 a share. The stock split 3-for-1 in 1998 and 4-for-1 in 1992.

DIVIDEND REINVESTMENT PLAN DETAILS

$1,000 to join plan (minimum will be waived if investor agrees to monthly investments of $100 via automatic withdrawal from checking accounts).

Optional cash payments of $100 monthly to $250,000 annually. The payments are invested weekly.

Figure 9-1. Disney (DIS)

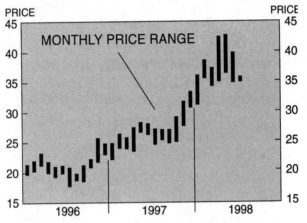

Exxon Corp.

5959 Las Calinas Blvd.
Irving, TX 75039
1-800-252-1800 (Plan Agent)
XON/New York Stock Exchange
Dividends paid since 1882
S&P earnings and dividend ranking: A
Indicated annual dividend as of June 30, 1998: $1.64
Increase in dividends from 1993 to indicated 1998: 14%
$10,000 invested on 12/31/87 worth on 12/31/97 with dividends reinvested: $48,523
Ten-year annualized total return: 19%

Every day, millions of motorists "put a tiger in their tanks" at some 32,000 Exxon or Esso service stations around the world. One of the world's largest companies by a number of measures, Exxon is involved in every phase of the petroleum industry, from exploring for and producing oil and natural gas in 26 countries to refining and marketing operations carried out in 76 countries. The company traces its roots to Standard Oil and its founder John D. Rockefeller.

Exxon is not just oil, however. The company boasts the world's third largest petrochemical operations and is one of the world's largest independent (nonutility) power producers. It also has a major presence in coal and minerals. Over the longer term, Exxon should benefit from increased natural gas sales to Latin America and the Pacific Rim because of expanding economies in those areas.

The company currently is second only to Royal Dutch Shell in terms of the size of its oil and gas reserves: 6.2 billion barrels of crude oil and 26.1 trillion cubic feet of natural gas as of the end of 1997. Debt accounts for a modest 18% of total capitalization, while internal cash generation is usually sufficient to fund capital spending. Earnings have grown at a 12% average annual rate over the past five years through 1997.

DIVIDEND REINVESTMENT PLAN DETAILS

$250 to join plan.

Optional cash payments of $50 per investment to $200,000 annually. The payments are invested weekly.

Automatic withdrawal from checking accounts is available.

Offers Individual Retirement Account.

Figure 9-2. Exxon Corp. (XON)

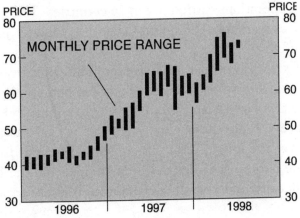

Lucent Technologies

600 Mountain Ave.
Murray Hill NJ 07974
1-888-582-3686 (Plan Agent)
LU/New York Stock Exchange
Indicated annual dividend as of June 30, 1998: $0.16
No long-term dividend information or S&P Quality ranking
available because company was recently spun off from AT&T.

Lucent Technologies, formerly a unit of AT&T, was spun off from the telephone giant in September 1996. The company is one of the world's leading designers, developers and manufacturers of telecommunications systems, software and products. It is a global market leader in the sale of public telecommunications systems and is a supplier of systems or software to most of the world's largest network operators.

Lucent is also a global market leader in the sale of business communications systems and in the sale of microelectronic components for communications applications to manufacturers of communications systems and computers. In addition, the company has provided engineering, installation and operations support services to more than 250 network operators in 75 countries, 1.4 million business locations in the U.S. and about 100,000 business locations in over 90 other countries.

R&D activities are conducted through Bell Laboratories, which consists of about 75% of the total resources of AT&T's former Bell Labs division. One recent result of these R&D activities was the introduction by Lucent's optical networking group of a new dense wavelength division multiplexing (DWDM) system that supports up to 80 optical channels at 2.5 gigabits per second over a single optical fiber. The company has acquired a number of businesses to fill in key positions in its messaging and data networking sector.

DIVIDEND REINVESTMENT PLAN DETAILS

$1,000 to join plan.

Optional cash payments of $100 per investment to $50,000 annually. The payments are invested daily.

Automatic withdrawal from checking accounts is available.

Offers Individual Retirement Account.

Figure 9-3. Lucent Technologies (LU)

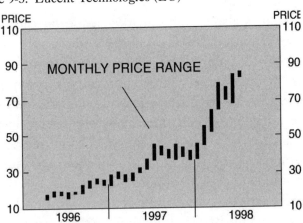

McDonald's Corp.

Campus Office Bldg.
Kroc Drive
Oakbrook, IL 60521
1-800-621-7825 (Plan Agent)

MCD/New York Stock Exchange
Dividends paid since 1976
S&P earnings and dividend ranking: A+
Indicated annual dividend as of June 30, 1998: $0.36
Increase in dividends from 1993 to indicated 1998: 71%
$10,000 invested on 12/31/87 worth on 12/31/97 with
dividends reinvested: $47,187
Ten-year annualized total return: 19%

One of the most recognized global brand names, McDonald's is the largest fast-food restaurant company in the U.S. and in the world. At the end of 1997, some 49% of its more than 23,000 restaurants were outside the U.S. Earnings, which have risen at an annual rate of 11% over the past five years, should continue to increase at a double-digit rate, paced by international operations.

In recent years, foreign operations have accounted for about 60% of total profits. Operating earnings from international restaurants should increase faster than domestic profits over the longer term. In foreign markets, additional benefits from economies of scale are likely as the company's presence continues to grow. In the U.S., the company has faced stiff competition. As a result, McDonald's has changed management and is focusing on productivity and lowering the overall cost structure. It also overhauled its food preparation service procedures to provide fresher, hotter food and to reduce labor costs.

The company has a large, ongoing share-repurchase program. Dividends, although modest, have jumped 157% since 1988.

DIVIDEND REINVESTMENT PLAN DETAILS

$1,000, or $100 per month via an automatic withdrawal plan from checking or savings accounts, to join plan.

Optional cash payments of $100 per investment to $250,000 annually may be made. The payments are invested weekly.

Offers Individual Retirement Account.

Figure 9-4. McDonald's Corp. (MCD)

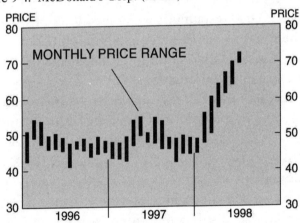

Procter & Gamble

1 Procter & Gamble Plaza
Cincinnati, OH 45202
1-800-742-6253

PG/New York Stock Exchange
Dividends paid since 1891
S&P earnings and dividend ranking: A
Indicated annual dividend as of June 30, 1998: $1.01
Increase in dividends from 1993 to indicated 1998: 84%
$10,000 invested on 12/31/87 worth on 12/31/97 with
dividends reinvested: $91,712
Ten-year annualized total return: 28%

With the likes of Crest toothpaste, Pampers disposable diapers and Tide detergent in its family of products, Procter & Gamble has amassed a portfolio of premier consumer brands in a variety of categories. PG manufactures and markets more than 300 brands of consumer products sold in 140 countries.

Management hopes to double unit volume in ten years, increase market share in the majority of the company's categories and provide shareholder returns that are in the top third of its peer group. The creation of new products and improvement in existing products are vital to PG's continued success. Tide Ultra II represents the latest of more than 60 performance improvements since the brand was first introduced in 1946. The food and beverage segment is adding production capacity for Olean, a fat substitute that was approved by the FDA in 1996.

The company is focusing on the successful implementation of value pricing and the maintenance of key customer relations in developing markets such as China, Mexico, Brazil, and Russia. In 1997, PG acquired Tambrands, the leading tampon producer in the U.S.

Over the longer term, earnings growth should outpace sales, and profits should climb more than 12% annually. Dividends, which have been boosted for 43 consecutive years, should also remain in an uptrend.

DIVIDEND REINVESTMENT PLAN DETAILS

$250 minimum investment to join plan.

Optional cash payments of $100 per investment to $120,000 annually may be made. The payments are invested weekly.

Automatic withdrawal from checking accounts is available.

Figure 9-5. Procter & Gamble (PG)

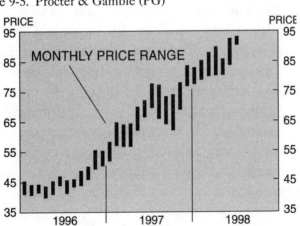

Regions Financial

417 North 20th St.
Birmingham AL 35202-0247
1-800-524-2879 (Plan Agent)

RGBK/Nasdaq
Dividends paid since 1968
S&P earnings and dividend ranking: A+
Indicated annual dividend as of June 30, 1998: $0.92
Increase in dividends from 1993 to indicated 1998: 77%
$10,000 invested on 12/31/87 worth on 12/31/97 with
dividends reinvested: $95,531
Ten-year annualized total return: 28%

Formerly First Alabama Bancshares, Regions Financial is a major southeastern bank holding company operating more than 430 offices in Alabama, Florida, Georgia, Louisiana, and Tennessee. This service territory is seeing economic growth higher than the national average.

Regions' goal is to become the best performing bank in the U.S. by 2000. The company has grown rapidly in recent years via internal growth and acquisitions. Aiding the expansion has been a quality loan portfolio and a relatively lean cost structure.

The company also operates nonbank subsidiaries that provide mortgage banking, credit life insurance, securities brokerage activities, and commercial accounts receivable factoring. The bank has a low chargeoff rate, thanks to Regions' conservative business mix.

Earnings have increased at an average annual rate of 8% over the past five years. Dividends have surged 156%

in the decade since 1988. Future earnings should be fueled by growth in non-interest income (various customer fees) and by a continued aggressive acquisition program. In the first quarter of 1998 alone, six acquisitions were completed. Three were in South Carolina and one each in Louisiana, Florida, and Georgia. As of April 1998, Regions had five pending transactions in Georgia, Alabama, Arkansas, and Florida.

DIVIDEND REINVESTMENT PLAN DETAILS

$1,000 minimum investment to join plan.

Optional cash payments of $25 per investment to $120,000 annually may be made. The payments are invested weekly.

Automatic withdrawal from checking or savings accounts is available.

Figure 9-6. Regions Financial (RGBK)

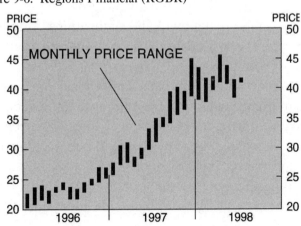

Group II: Stocks with Outstanding Dividend Growth

The six stocks that follow, all taken from Table 3-2 on pages 65-69, have outstanding records of dividend growth. Each has increased its payments to shareholders by at least 200% over the last decade. Investors should consider these issues as excellent long-term holdings. Even if you are close to or in retirement, your portfolio generally should contain companies that rapidly increase their dividend payments. Over time, you will be better off than if you buy companies that have high current yield but provide little in the way of dividend growth. As we saw in Chapter 3, stocks with strong dividend growth can offset the effects of inflation.

Automatic Data Processing

One ADP Blvd.
Roseland, NJ 07068
(973) 994-5000

AUD/New York Stock Exchange
Dividends paid since 1974
S&P earnings & dividend ranking: A+
Indicated annual dividend as of June 30, 1998: $0.53
Increase in dividends from 1993 through indicated 1998: 121%
$10,000 invested on 12/31/87 worth on 12/31/97 with
dividends reinvested: $60,252
Ten-year annualized total return: 22%

One of the largest independent computer services firms in the world, Automatic Data Processing derives over $4 billion in annual revenues from more than 400,000 clients. The company, which was founded in 1949, operates in four business segments. The largest is employer services, which accounted for some 55% of revenues in fiscal 1997 (ended June). Payroll services, which handles paychecks for 23 million people and supplies W-2 forms for 35 million, contributed about 85% of the segment's revenues. The company's second largest business segment is brokerage services. Automatic Data processes roughly 20% of the retail stock transactions in the U.S. and Canada, handling more than 475,000 trades a day. ADP's two other business segments are dealer services for the automobile industry and claims services for the property and casualty insurance industry.

Through March 1998, Automatic Data posted 147 consecutive quarters of higher sales and earnings. For 36 years in a row, the company has increased per-share earnings at a double-digit rate. Customer loyalty is a principal reason for this outstanding record. ADP has a client-retention rate of more than 90%. In late 1995, ADP acquired Paris-based GSI Group, which has operations in France, Germany, Italy, Spain, Switzerland, and the United Kingdom. As a result of that acquisition ADP has become the leading provider of payroll and human resources information services in Europe.

In November 1997, Automatic Data Processing increased its dividend for the 24th consecutive year.

Figure 9-7. Automatic Data Processing (AUD)

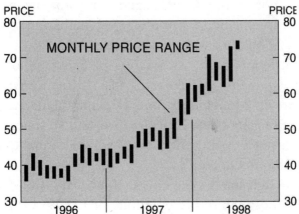

Glacier Bancorp

202 Main St.
Kalispell, MT 59901
(406) 756-4200

GBCI/Nasdaq
Dividends paid since 1985
S&P earnings & dividend ranking: A+
Indicated annual dividend as of June 30, 1998: $0.52
Increase in dividends from 1993 through indicated 1998: 89%
$10,000 invested on 12/31/87 worth on 12/31/97 with
dividends reinvested: $180,275
Ten-year annualized total return: 38%
A dividend reinvestment plan is available.

By most measures, giant Citicorp and tiny Glacier Bancorp are not in the same league. Citicorp, the holding company for one of the world's largest banks, has assets of about $252 billion and operates more than 3,000 offices in 98 countries. Glacier, with assets of $580 million, is a holding company that operates just 18 branches, all of which are in Montana. In one very important measure, however, Glacier beats Citicorp: Over the 10 years ended 1997, Glacier's stock provided an average annual total return of 38% to Citicorp's 29%.

Although small, Glacier is a strong bank. In 1997, the company posted a return on equity of 17.67% vs. 15.86% a year earlier. Return on assets was 1.63% vs. 1.43% in 1996. For the 1997 year, commercial loan growth was 21%. Despite robust growth in its loan portfolio, Glacier is a careful lender. The bank's non-performing loans amounted to 0.31% of loans vs. 0.85% for its peer group.

Investors seeking dividends should like this bank. It went public in 1984, began paying a dividend the following year, and has increased it each year since. At the end of 1997, the company paid an extra dividend of $0.05 a share in addition to its regular $0.12 annual dividend.

Figure 9-8. Glacier Bancorp (GBCI)

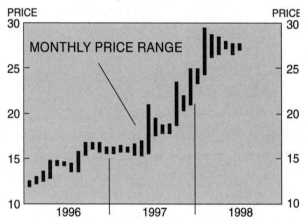

Home Depot

2727 Paces Ferry Rd.
Atlanta, GA 30339
(770)433-8211

HD/New York Stock Exchange
Dividends paid since 1987
S&P earnings and dividend ranking: A+
Indicated annual dividend as of June 30, 1998: $0.12
Increase in dividends from 1993 to indicated 1998: 300%
$10,000 invested on 12/31/87 worth on 12/31/97 with
dividends reinvested: $328,037
Ten-year annualized return: 47%
A dividend reinvestment plan is available.

Founded in 1978, Home Depot is the world's largest home improvement retailer. As of mid-year 1998, it had garnered some 14% of the U.S. $140 billion home improvement industry. The company operates retail warehouse-type stores selling a wide assortment of building materials and home improvement products, primarily to the do-it-yourself and home remodeling markets. It currently operates 625 stores in 44 states, mostly in California, Florida, and Texas, and 32 stores in Canada.

Stores average 105,000 square feet, plus 20,000 square feet to 28,000 square feet of garden center and storage space. The stores stock 40,000 to 50,000 product items. Home Depot aims to provide a broad range of merchandise at competitive prices. Growth opportunities remain in existing and as yet untapped markets in the U.S. The company plans to expand its square footage base by

21% to 22% annually, which will take it to over 1,300 stores by the end of 2001.

The EXPO design centers, which sell upscale interior design products, are a test concept. Five units were operating in mid-year 1998, with two more expected to be added by the end of 1999.

The company expanded to Canada in 1994, with the acquisition of a 75% interest in Aikenhead's home improvement warehouse chain. Beginning in 2000, it has the right to acquire the remaining 25%. Expansion to Latin America has begun and stores in other foreign countries are also planned. The company's per-share profits have grown at an annual rate of 20% over the past five years.

Figure 9-9. Home Depot (HD)

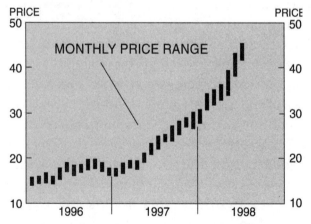

Merck & Co.

One Merck Drive
P.O. Box 100
Whitehouse Station, NJ 08889
(908) 423-1000

MRK/New York Stock Exchange
Dividends paid since 1935
S&P earnings and dividend ranking: A+
Indicated annual dividend as of June 30, 1998: $1.80
Increase in dividends from 1993 to indicated 1998: 70%
$10,000 invested on 12/31/87 worth on 12/31/97 with
dividends reinvested: $74,245
Ten-year annualized total return: 25%
A dividend reinvestment plan is available.

One of the world's premier pharmaceutical research companies (R&D spending amounts to $1.7 billion), Merck has concentrated its efforts on creating breakthrough drugs to treat chronic illnesses. Key products in late-stage clinical trials include treatments for migraine, asthma, and unstable angina. The company recently discovered a new class of anti-infectives aimed at drug-resistant bacteria, which could revolutionize the antibiotics market.

Merck is a leader in the vast market for high-margin cardiovascular drugs, with five drugs generating aggregate sales of more than $9 billion in 1997. Key products include cholesterol-lowering agents such as Zocor and Mevacor and treatments for high blood pressure and congestive heart failure like Vasotec/Vaseretic, Prinivil/Prinzide and Cozaar/Hyzaar, the first of a new class of antihypertensives. The company has an estimated 40% share of the rapidly growing worldwide cholesterol reduction market and about one-third of the hypertension-angina market. Merck's new drug, Vioxx, has blockbuster potential. Studies have shown Vioxx improved the ability of osteoarthritis patients to perform routine daily tasks.

As Merck's research thrived, so did its shareholders. Had you purchased Merck shares at their average price in 1988, your dividend a decade later would have provided a 10% yield on your original investment. We expect Merck to continue to do well. Although politicians like to criticize drug companies for the cost of their medications, often drug therapy is significantly less expensive than alternatives.

Figure 9-10. Merck & Co. (MRK)

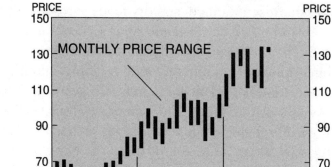

Sysco Corp.

1390 Enclave Parkway
Houston, TX 77077
(281) 584-1390

SYY/New York Stock Exchange
Dividends paid since 1970
S&P earnings and dividend ranking: A+
Indicated annual dividend as of June 30, 1998: $0.36
Increase in dividends from 1993 to indicated 1998: 177%
$10,000 invested on 12/31/87 worth on 12/31/97 with
dividends reinvested: $74,272
Ten-year annualized total return: 25%
A dividend reinvestment plan is available.

This company is the giant of the U.S. food service distribution industry, selling products to more than 270,000 customers in the "dining-out" industry. Sysco sells a full line of fresh, frozen, canned, and dry foods to restaurants, cafeterias, and other out-of-home food servers. In addition to foods, the company distributes paper products, tableware, kitchen equipment, and cleaning supplies. Products include both national brands and goods packed under Sysco's private label. The company's broader line of product offerings includes such items as fresh meats, imported specialties, and fresh produce. It operates from 69 distribution centers throughout the continental U.S., Alaska, and parts of Canada.

Although it is the food service distribution industry leader, Sysco still has room to grow; it controls only about 10% of the highly-fragmented $140 billion industry.

About 60% of the company's customers are restaurants, while hospitals and nursing homes are another 12%.

We expect the domestic food service industry to continue growing at about 3% a year as Americans, always pressed for time, take more of their meals away from home. Sysco's per-share earnings growth should be 12% to 15% annually over the next few years as the company gains market share at the expense of its weaker rivals and continues its share-buyback program. Dividends, up 679% in the ten years 1988 to 1998 (indicated), should increase regularly.

Figure 9-11. Sysco Corp. (SYY)

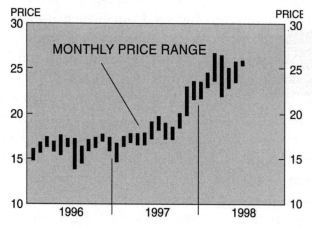

Travelers Group

388 Greenwich St.
New York, NY 10013
(212) 816-8000
TRV/New York Stock Exchange
Dividends paid since 1986
S&P earnings & dividend ranking: A+
Indicated annual dividend as of June 30, 1998: $0.50
Increase in dividends from 1993 through indicated 1998: 213%
$10,000 invested on 12/31/87 worth on 12/31/97 with dividends reinvested: $163,480
Ten-year annualized total return: 36%

Although the company's name has changed from Primerica Corp. to Travelers Inc. (and will change again to Citigroup after its merger with Citicorp, which was approved as we went to press), Travelers Group has been much more consistent in its returns to investors. A $10,000 investment in the stock a decade earlier had grown to be worth more than 16 times as much by the end of 1997.

The financial services giant is one of the top securities brokers via its Salomon Smith Barney unit. In 1997, Salomon Smith Barney was the leading underwriter of municipal debt and the second largest global debt and equity underwriter. In 1998, the company acquired a 25% equity interest in Tokyo-based Nikko Securities for $1.6 billion. Travelers Group also provides life, accident and health, and property-casualty insurance, as well as annuities and mutual funds.

The merger with Citicorp will create a vast banking and financial services empire with assets of almost $700 billion and earnings of more than $7.5 billion. Although current law prohibits bank holding companies from underwriting insurance, Travelers has received a two-year waiver, which may be extended for three additional one-year periods.

The long-term success of the merger will depend on the new Citigroup's ability to cut costs and sell its various financial products to current customers of both Citicorp and Travelers. Given the company's track record, the odds appear to be in its favor.

Figure 9-12. Travelers Group (TRV)

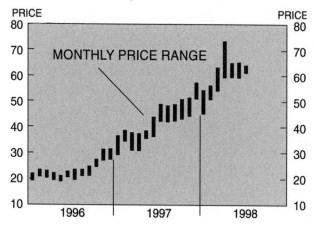

Group III: Top Quality Stocks

The following is a suggested portfolio for more conservative investors. All six of the stocks carry Standard & Poor's highest earnings and dividend ranking of A+, indicating at least a decade of superior earnings and dividend growth and stability.

The letter rankings (commonly called "quality rankings") are historical and are not intended to predict stock price movement. By their nature, however, many issues ranked A+ have low volatility and hold out the promise of good long-term performance. Therefore, the issues are generally suitable for conservative investors with a longer time horizon.

Albertson's

250 Parkcenter Blvd.
P.O. Box 20
Boise, ID 83726
(208) 385-6200

ABS/New York Stock Exchange
Dividends paid since 1960
Indicated annual dividend as of June 30, 1998: $0.68
Increase in dividends from 1988 to indicated 1998: 267%
$10,000 invested on 12/31/87 worth on 12/31/97 with
dividends reinvested: $85,528
Ten-year annualized total return: 27%
A dividend reinvestment plan is available.

With more than 950 stores in 22 western, midwestern and southern states and annual sales approaching $15 billion, Albertson's is one of the largest food and drug retailers in the U.S. The company is not content to stand still, however. Over the next five years, it expects to open about 380 new stores and remodel 290 existing ones. It also is being more aggressive when looking at acquisitions. For example, in January 1998, two separate deals added a total of 53 stores in both new and existing markets.

The majority of Albertson's stores are combination food-drug stores that range in size from 35,000 to 82,000 square feet. The company also operates 38 warehouse stores under the Max Food and Drug name. These no-frills stores average 17,000 to 73,000 square feet.

Albertson's long-term objective is to increase earnings at a 15% annual rate. Profits over the past five years have grown 9% annually. In addition to new store development, the company intends to increase sales and profits by offering a number of customer-focused programs aimed at meeting the changing needs of busy consumers by adding value to their shopping trip. These initiatives include "Quick Fixin' Ideas," which consist of heat-and-serve entrees in the service deli and complete meal recipes and value-added products in the produce, meat and frozen food departments, expansion of the pharmacy business, and the addition of special services such as in-store banking.

Figure 9-13. Albertson's (ABS)

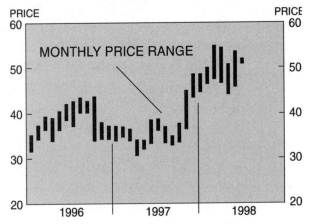

Coca-Cola Co.

1 Coca-Cola Plaza N.W.
Atlanta, GA 30313
(404) 676-2121

KO/New York Stock Exchange
Dividends paid since 1893
Indicated annual dividend as of June 30, 1998: $0.60
Increase in dividends from 1988 to indicated 1998: 253%
$10,000 invested on 12/31/1987 worth on 12/31/1997 with
dividends reinvested: $162,112
Ten-year annualized total return: 36%
A dividend reinvestment plan is available.

Coca-Cola, the world's largest soft drink producer, is the most recognized brand name in the world. Soft drink products bearing the company's trademarks have been sold since 1886. A major factor behind Coke's solid earnings and dividend record has been its aggressive pursuit of less-developed markets around the world. Coke does business in 200 countries, deriving nearly 70% of total revenues and about 80% of operating profits from regions outside the more mature U.S. market. That gives the company substantial insulation from the inevitable economic downturns of any one region.

In addition, with per-capita consumption of soft drink products outside the U.S. at less than 15% of the U.S. level, there is strong longer-term growth potential. Coca-Cola's huge infrastructure gives it the resources and competitive advantage to realize this potential. The company has equity positions in more than 30 unconsolidated bottling and distribution operations.

The company's strategy is to leverage 8% to 10% annual gallon shipment growth into high-teen earnings-per-share growth through a combination of concentrate price increases, volume-based efficiencies and share repurchases.

Standard & Poor's expects Coca-Cola's rapid earnings growth, high return on invested capital, dependable dividend growth, and strong balance sheet to continue to make the stock an attractive long-term portfolio holding.

Figure 9-14. Coca-Cola Co. (KO)

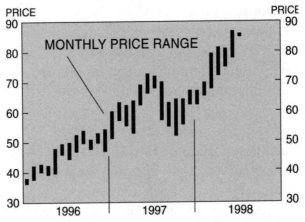

General Electric

3135 Easton Turnpike
Fairfield CT 06431
(203)373-2211

GE/New York Stock Exchange
Dividends paid since 1899
Indicated annual dividend as of June 30, 1998: $1.20
Increase in dividends from 1993 to indicated 1998: 90%
$10,000 invested on 12/31/87 worth on 12/31/97 with
dividends reinvested: $85,157
Ten-year annualized return: 27%
A dividend reinvestment plan is available.

A diverse company, General Electric's interests include a broad range of services, technology and manufacturing. Management's goal is to be first or second in terms of market share in each business. Businesses that are not leaders are divested.

Quality, globalization, service, information technology, and consumer wealth accumulation and protection have been major themes. Initiatives have been successful in boosting quality and lowering costs. GE is moving rapidly into growing global markets, which has resulted in overseas revenues accounting for more than 40% of revenues and more than 30% of profits.

The company aims to capture a larger part of the recurring revenue stream tied to aftermarket service of manufactured products. This strategy is having the greatest effect in GE's aircraft engines, medical equipment, power generation and locomotives businesses. Information technology includes developing GE's media and satellite leasing businesses, as well as applying advanced communications techniques in all units to improve their competitiveness. Consumer wealth accumulation addresses the growing demand for financial, insurance, health care, and other needs of aging baby boomers.

GE operates in two groups: (1) product, service and media businesses and (2) GE Capital Services. The first group consists of 11 businesses: aircraft engines, appliances, lighting, medical systems, NBC broadcasting, plastics, power systems, electrical distribution and control, information services, motors and industrial systems and transportation systems. Capital services includes 27 financial businesses clustered in equipment management, speciality insurance, consumer services, specialized financing and mid-market financing. Earnings have grown at an average annual rate of 14% over the past five years.

Figure 9-15. General Electric (GE)

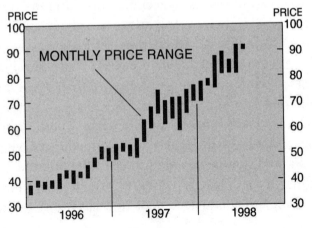

Gillette Co.

Prudential Tower Bldg.
Boston, MA 02199
(617) 421-7000

G/New York Stock Exchange
Dividends paid since 1906
Indicated annual dividend as of June 30, 1998: $0.51
Increase in dividends from 1988 to indicated 1998: 337%
$10,000 invested on 12/31/1987 worth on 12/31/1997 with
dividends reinvested: $162,612
Ten-year annualized total return: 36%
A dividend reinvestment plan is available.

This well-known global maker of razors and blades, hair care products, toiletries, writing instruments, and small appliances has recorded strong earnings growth, a high return on equity and an impressive return on sales over the years. Popular brand names include Braun, Right Guard, White Rain, Silkience, Parker Pen, Papermate, and Oral-B. Gillette's businesses are number one in their markets.

Profit margins of the company's largest business, blades and razors, continue to widen on higher volume and a better mix. The greatest volume growth is occurring in international markets, as the company expands its presence in untapped regions, especially in Asia and Latin America. The company's new Mach3 shaving system, introduced in mid-1998, has done well.

Gillette's acquisition in 1996 of Duracell International, the world's leading maker of high-performance alkaline batteries with a 40% world market share, has proven to be a successful move. In the spring of 1998, Duracell introduced a new line of alkaline batteries designed to last 50% longer in high drain devices such as digital cameras and laptop computers. Over the next several years, Duracell should contribute the fastest earnings growth to Gillette.

Figure 9-16. Gillette Co. (G)

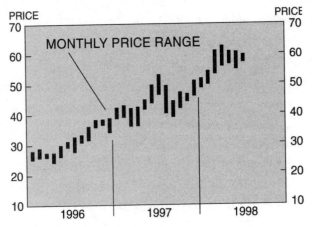

Johnson & Johnson

One Johnson & Johnson Plaza
New Brunswick, NJ 08933
(732) 524-0400

JNJ/New York Stock Exchange
Dividends paid since 1944
Indicated annual dividend as of June 30, 1998: $1.00
Increase in dividends from 1988 to indicated 1998: 257%
$10,000 invested on 12/31/87 worth on 12/31/97 with
dividends reinvested: $83,920
Ten-year annualized total return: 27%
A dividend reinvestment plan is available.

The world's largest health care company's commanding positions in rapidly expanding medical markets point to continued strong earnings growth for the foreseeable future.

Some of the more noteworthy fast-growing product lines developed in recent years have been Risperdal antipsychotic and Sporanox antifungal drugs and the Life-Scan home glucose monitoring system. These and similar products enabled Johnson & Johnson to rack up annual earnings growth of more than 14% from 1992 to 1997. Foreign business accounts for more than 45% of sales and 35% of profits.

Although usually thought of as a medical products and hospital supplies firm, JNJ derives close to 60% of profits from a growing list of drugs. More than 80 different prescription drug, contraceptive and veterinary products are sold, 20 of which generate revenues in excess of

$100 million. Some of the best sellers include Procrit red blood stimulant, Propulsid gastrointestinal, Risperdal anti-psychotic and Ortho-Novum oral contraceptive. Promising new products include Ergoset, a drug for Type II diabetes and obesity, and Aciphex for gastroesophageal reflux disease.

The company's long list of consumer products (including Tylenol analgesic, Band-Aid adhesives and Johnson's baby powder), although showing slower growth, provides a solid base of stability and cash flow.

Figure 9-17. Johnson & Johnson (JNJ)

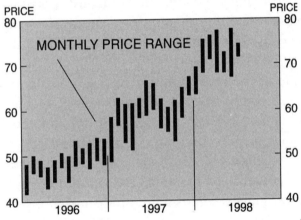

Wilmington Trust

Rodney Sq. North
Wilmington, DE 19890
(302) 651-1000

WILM/Nasdaq
Dividends paid since 1914
Indicated annual dividend as of June 30, 1998: $1.56
Increase in dividends from 1988 to indicated 1998: 239%
$10,000 invested on 12/31/87 worth on 12/31/97 with
dividends reinvested: $66,921
Ten-year annualized total return: 24%
A dividend reinvestment plan is available.

This bank holding company, through its Wilmington Trust subsidiary, operates more than 60 branches offering a broad variety of financial services, mainly in Delaware. Over the past five years, the company has posted returns on assets and equity well in excess of industry averages. Wilmington Trust's strong reputation as a fiduciary and investment manager has made it one of the most consistently profitable firms in the industry.

As one of the largest personal trust institutions in the U.S., Wilmington offers trust administration, investment management, private banking, custody, estate and financial planning, and estate settlement services for its clients. Delaware's favorable tax and legal environment also enables the company to be a major provider of trust and administrative services to corporations. In addition, Wilmington provides institutional investment advisory services to clients throughout the U.S. and offers a proprietary family of Rodney Square Mutual Funds.

Noninterest income should continue to show strong growth, driven by trust and asset management fees as Wilmington opens offices and looks to gain market share in key wealth centers such as New York City and parts of California. In late 1997, the company agreed to acquire a 24% ownership of Carmer Rosenthal McGlynn, which is an investment adviser for wealthy individuals, as well as for foundations, endowments and pension plans.

Figure 9-18. Wilmington Trust (WILM)

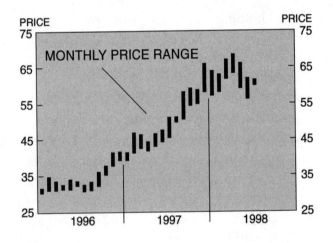

Group IV: Higher-Yielding Stocks for Current Income

As we write this in July 1998, the following five stocks have dividend yields at least three times the 1.4% yield of the S&P 500. Investors seeking current income may find these issues attractive. Often that means retired individuals who count on stock dividends to pay some of their living costs. As people live longer, the number of years the average person spends in retirement increases. Consequently, we believe that even retired people will do better over time with lower-yielding stocks that raise their dividends rapidly. Even if you do need investment income for regular expenses, add some low-yielding, growing-dividend stocks (see Group II) to your portfolio mix.

Baltimore Gas & Electric

P.O. Box 1475
Baltimore, MD 21203
(800) 685-0123

BGE/New York Stock Exchange
Dividends paid since 1910
S&P earnings & dividend ranking: B+
Indicated annual dividend as of June 30, 1998: $1.68
Increase in dividends from 1993 through indicated 1998: 14%
$10,000 invested on 12/31/87 worth on 12/31/97 with
dividends reinvested: $31,224
Ten-year annualized total return: 13%

This electric and gas utility provides power to more than 1.6 million customers in Baltimore and central Maryland. In December 1997, the company terminated a planned merger with neighboring Potomac Electric Power. Both companies determined that financial conditions imposed on their proposed merger by Public Service Commissions in Maryland and the District of Columbia were not in the best interests of their shareholders.

Deregulation of the power industry is coming to BGE's service territory, as it is in most areas of the country. Staring in July 2000, some customers will be able to choose their electric supplier. Full deregulation will take two years. BGE appears to be in a fairly good position to weather deregulation since only about 10% of its customer revenues are industrial. Industrial customers are often most aggressive in seeking alternative energy suppliers. Residential customers provide about 42% of the utility's revenues.

BGE will obtain more financial flexibility now that Maryland legislators have pledged to end the state's ban on utility holding companies. Holding company status will enable BGE to fund the growth of its non-regulated businesses, which could provide the company with stronger growth opportunities. Regulated utilities can't directly subsidize non-regulated subsidiaries.

Over the last decade, BGE has increased its dividend by 27%. In mid-1998, the stock had a yield of 5.4% vs. a 4.2% yield for the S&P utilities index. With a dividend that appears secure, the shares should provide above-average current income and moderate total return.

Figure 9-19. Baltimore Gas & Electric (BGE)

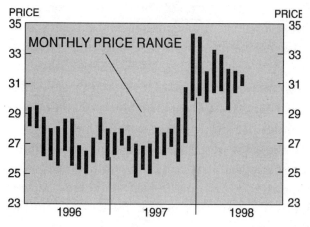

Meditrust

197 First Ave.
Needham Heights, MA 02194
(617) 433-6000

MT/New York Stock Exchange
Dividends paid since 1986
S&P earnings and dividend ranking: NR
Indicated annual dividend as of June 30, 1998: $2.45
Increase in dividends from 1988 to indicated 1998: 27%
$10,000 invested on 12/31/87 worth on 12/31/97 with
dividends reinvested: $43,834
Ten-year annualized total return: 18%
A dividend reinvestment plan is available.

Meditrust Corp., the result of the 1997 combination of Meditrust and the much smaller Santa Anita Companies, is the largest health care real estate investment trust in the U.S. As a paired-shared REIT (both owner and operator), Meditrust consists of two companies, Meditrust Corp. and Meditrust Operating Co., that trade together as a pair under the single ticker symbol.

At the end of 1997, nursing homes accounted for 51% of Meditrust's investments, while assisted living facilities, designed to provide custodial care and to supplement hospital care, accounted for 21% of investments. Rehabilitation facilities, medical offices, and acute care hospitals accounted for the rest.

The company is expected to spend about $500 million in real estate acquisitions in 1998. The majority of investments will be concentrated in nursing homes and assisted living centers. In addition, Meditrust bought a hotel company, La Quinta Inns, for $3 billion in stock and cash in an effort to diversify out of health-care-related real estate. Rental revenues could benefit over the long term from escalatory clauses specified in certain leases.

Funds from operations, or cash flow (an important measure of operating performance for a REIT), should continue to increase in the years ahead, as well as dividend hikes (a REIT must pay out at least 95% of its net taxable income in dividends)

The shares have fallen sharply from their late 1997 high as investors overreacted to new restrictions on operations of paired-share REITs. Meditrust's current operations won't be affected by the new regulations.

Figure 9-20. Meditrust

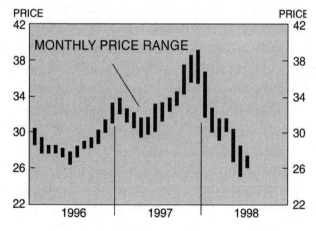

Middlesex Water

P.O. Box 1500
Iselin, NJ 08830
(732) 634-1500

MSEX/Nasdaq
Dividends paid since 1912
S&P earnings & dividend ranking: A–
Indicated annual dividend as of June 30, 1998: $1.14
Increase in dividends from 1993 through indicated 1998: 13%
$10,000 invested on 12/31/87 worth on 12/31/97 with
dividends reinvested: $33,607
Ten-year annualized total return: 14%

With deregulation causing upheavals in the electric, gas, and telephone industries, water utilities are an island of calm in the investment world. Middlesex Water is one such island. The company provides metered water service to some 54,000 households in a 55-square-mile area of New Jersey that has a total population of about 212,000 people. In addition, through a subsidiary, the company provides water to 6,600 households containing a population of 23,000 in Delaware. The company provides water and water treatment to an additional 2,200 households in New Jersey.

In January 1998, Middlesex received approval from the New Jersey Board of Public Utilities (BPU) for a $1.5 million (4.4%) overall rate increase. The rate boost will provide the utility with an allowed rate of return on equity of 11% and an overall rate of return of 8.56%. The BPU also approved issuance of $23 million of tax-exempt New

Jersey Economic Development Authority bonds. Proceeds will be used to upgrade a company water treatment plant to assure compliance with increased drinking water standards and to provide added capacity.

As a regulated utility, Middlesex Water will not provide spectacular share price gains. Over the last decade, the shares have risen only about 55%. But the company steadily increases its dividend, which recently provided a yield of 5.5%. If you are looking for current income, shares of this water company are worth considering.

Figure 9-21. Middlesex Water (MSEX)

Southern Co.

270 Peachtree St., N.W.
Atlanta, GA 30303
(770) 393-0650

SO/New York Stock Exchange
Dividends paid since 1948
S&P earnings and dividend ranking: A–
Indicated annual dividend as of June 30, 1998: $1.34
Increase in dividends from 1988 to indicated 1998: 25%
$10,000 invested on 12/31/87 worth on 12/31/97 with
dividends reinvested: $42,656
Ten-year annualized total return: 17%
A dividend reinvestment plan is available.

The Southern Company is the largest U.S. producer of electricity and one of the largest independent power producers in the world. The company serves 3.7 million customers in the southeastern U.S. through its domestic subsidiaries Alabama Power, Georgia Power, Gulf Power, Mississippi Power, and Savannah Electric & Power. It also serves 1.3 million customers in southwestern England through South Western Electricity. Although Southern owns 49% of South Western, it holds a majority of the voting shares and exercises operational control.

In 1997, Southern acquired Consolidated Electric Power Asia, the fifth largest independent power producer in the world. The Hong Kong-based company has electric power generating projects either completed or under development in China, the Philippines, Indonesia, Pakistan, and India.

In 1997, the company also acquired 26% of Berliner Kraft und Licht AG, a vertically integrated electric utility serving 2.1 million customers in Berlin. The transaction provided Southern with an entry into a strong and growing economy and access to transmission lines connecting to other parts of Europe.

Southern intends to become one of the five top energy marketers in the U.S. by 2000, and expects its non-core operations to grow to about 30% of net income by 2003.

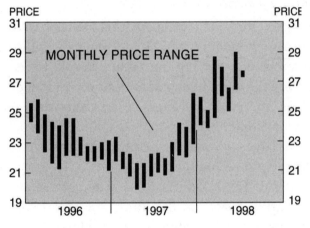

Figure 9-22. Southern Co. (SO)

Texas Utilities

1601 Bryan St.
Dallas, TX 75201
(214) 812-4600

TXU/New York Stock Exchange
Dividends paid since 1917
S&P earnings & dividend ranking: B
Indicated annual dividend as of June 30, 1998: $2.20
Change in dividends from 1993 through indicated 1998: -28%
$10,000 invested on 12/31/87 worth on 12/31/97 with
dividends reinvested: $31,646
Ten-year annualized total return: 14%

Through its principal subsidiary, this Dallas-based hold-ing company provides electricity to some six million peo-ple, or about one-third of the population of Texas. With strong growth in the telecommunications and electronics industries, the company's service area showed a 2% in-crease in customers in 1997. Texas Utilities also operates the fourth largest phone service provider in the state, with 100,000 telephone lines.

But it is Texas Utilities' recent energy acquisitions that will drive growth in the future. In May 1998, TXU bought Energy Group, which provides electricity to three million British customers. In 1997, it acquired Lone Star Gas, one of the largest gas distribution companies in the U.S., and Lone Star Pipeline, which has 7,600 miles of gathering and transmission pipelines in Texas. The Lone Star properties will enable the company to deliver com-prehensive energy services in an economically attractive area of the U.S. The company's recent acquisition activity began in late 1995, when it took control of Eastern Energy, a distribution company providing electric service to more than 480,000 customers in southeastern Australia.

As we noted in Chapter 8, Texas Utilities helped to fund its acquisitions by cutting its dividend by 35% in 1995. Since the company indicated that it wanted to conserve cash for acquisitions, the market responded positively and the share price advanced about 15% through mid-1998. The company has begun increasing its dividend since the cut. The January 1998 payment was almost 5% higher than the October 1997 quarterly dividend.

Figure 9-23. Texas Utilities (TXU)

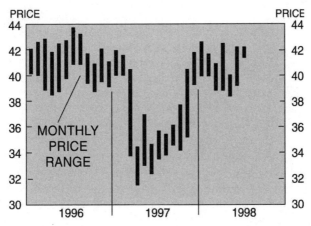

Where to Find Helpful Information

Information from many of the following sources can be found at larger public libraries. In addition, full-service brokers will be happy to provide you with earnings estimates or data on a company's recent dividend history. If you deal with a discount broker, you may have to pay a small fee for reports that cover these items.

Basic Company Information

Public companies must file a great deal of information with the **Securities and Exchange Commission (SEC)**. If you have a computer with a modem and browser software, you can access company filings through EDGAR, the SEC's online service at: **http://www.sec.gov.**

If you don't have a computer, or would prefer to deal with a print version of the information, contact the investor relations department of the company you want to know about. Request the latest annual report, 10-K report (issued annually, it's more detailed and more valuable than the regular annual) and most recent 10-Q report (a quarterly). For addresses or phone numbers of companies, contact the exchange or market on which the firm's stock trades.

The American Stock Exchange Fact Book has addresses and phone numbers of all ASE-listed issues. Send a check or money order for $20 (New York State residents: $21.65, including sales tax) to:

Publications Dept.
American Stock Exchange
86 Trinity Place
New York, NY 10006

You can call the ASE with a request for a listed company's address and phone number at **(212) 306-1490.** Computer users may obtain the information from the American Stock Exchange's website: **http://www.amex.com.**

The National Association of Securities Dealers (NASD), which operates the Nasdaq market (known to older investors as the over-the-counter market), also has a **Fact Book** that lists company addresses and phone numbers. The $20 book is available from NASD Media-Source. Credit card holders call **(301)-590-6578.** NASD will handle phone inquiries for addresses and phone numbers of Nasdaq-traded companies. Call the market research department at **202-728-8015**. Or you can access NASD's website at **http://nasdaq.com.**

The New York Stock Exchange's research department will provide you with phone numbers of up to five NYSE-listed companies at no charge. Call the NYSE at **(212) 656-3218.** Information on many NYSE-listed companies is available on the Exchange's Website at **http://www.nyse.com.**

Consensus Earnings Estimates

First Call has earnings estimates for close to 6,000 U.S. companies, available online, by fax, or in print. The print version, **First Call Consensus Estimate Guide,** is a monthly publication that sells for $250 a year. Single copy is $25. Call **800-448-2348.** The estimates are sold through a **fax-on-demand** service. Prices vary, but you can obtain a free sample by calling **800-418-3333** using a touch-tone phone. First Call estimates are also available through the company's website at **http://www.firstcall.com** for $1.50 to $3 each.

I/B/E/S offers consensus estimates on more than 5,000 U.S. companies. Via **CompuServe,** I/B/E/S estimates are $0.50 each or $2.50 for a more detailed report. The I/B/E/S estimates are also available by telephone for $2 per minute. **Call 900-225-2622.** Online access: **http://www.IBES.com.**

Dividend, Earnings, and Share Price Histories

Standard & Poor's Stock Reports provide a detailed look at any of 4,600 stocks. Touch-tone phone users may obtain reports by **fax or mail.** A basic two-page Stock Report is $6 and quantity discounts are available. For a free sample, call **800-292-0808.** Historical information on stocks is also available on Standard & Poor's website S&P Personal Wealth: **http://www.personalwealth.com.** Some of the information is available free. Other sections are open to registered users (still free, but you must register). To access S&P's personalized investment recommendations, you must be a Personal Wealth subscriber. You can take a one-month free trial subscription, after which the service costs $9.95 a month.

The Value Line Investment Survey is a weekly publication providing data on 1,700 stocks. A full year's subscription is $570; a 10-week trial is $55. Call **800-833-0046.**

Dividend Aristocrats

Higher Annual Dividend for at Least 25 Years

Each of the companies in this table has paid its shareholders a higher dividend every year for at least a quarter century. This is not a complete list, just a representative sample.

Table B-1

Company/Ticker	Industry	Number of Years Paid Higher Div.
American Business Products/ABP	Business Products	40
American Home Products/AHP	Health Care	47
Betz Laboratories/BTL	Chemicals	33
Black Hills Corp./BKH	Utilities	28

Table B-1 *(cont'd)*

Company/Ticker	Industry	Number of Years Paid Higher Div.
CCB Financial/CCB	Financial Services	34
Coca-Cola Co./KO	Food/Beverage	36
Commerce Bancshares/CBSH	Financial Services	30
Emerson Electric/EMR	Electrical Equipment	42
Frontier Corp./FRO	Telecommunications	39
H.J. Heinz/HNZ	Food/Beverage	31
Harcourt General/H	Diversified	30
HSB Group/HSB	Financial Services	33
Hormel Foods/HRL	Food/Beverage	32
International Flavors & Fragrances/IFF	Chemicals	38
Johnson & Johnson/JNJ	Health Care	36
Kellogg Co./K	Food/Beverage	42
Lilly (Eli)/LLY	Health Care	30
Marsh & McLennan Cos./MMC	Financial Services	35
Masco Corp./MAS	Building Products	40
Ohio Casualty/OCAS	Financial Services	52
PepsiCo/PEP	Food/Beverage	27
Pfizer, Inc./PFE	Health Care	31
Procter & Gamble/PG	Household Products	43
Rubbermaid, Inc./RBD	Household Products	47
Southtrust Corp./SOTR	Financial Services	29
Torchmark/TMK	Financial Services	48
Wisconsin Energy/WEC	Utilities	38

Index

Which Stocks Will Be Tomorrow's STARS?

Drawing on the vast experience of Standard & Poor's renowned staff of equities researchers and analysts, The OUTLOOK identifies the developments that affect stock performance — and makes recommendations on when to buy, hold and sell. The outstanding features include:

- *Market Forecast and Investment Policy* — a weekly forecast of where the market is headed, and what moves you should make.

- *Supervised Master List of Recommended Issues* — Standard & Poor's favorites for long-term capital appreciation and for superior long-term total return, plus the new Conservative and Aggressive Small/Mid-Cap Master Lists.

- *Plus STARS — One of Standard & Poor's Most Powerful Investment Decision-Making Tools!*
  The highly regarded *Stock Appreciation Ranking System* offers an easy way to pick stocks that Standard & Poor's believes will do best in the near term — six months to one year. Week after week, STARS ranks 1,100 active stocks from One to Five STARS, so you can track changes at a glance.

MAIL COUPON TODAY FOR A FREE ONE-MONTH SUBSCRIPTION!